"Practical, useful, and completely readable. Bill Knaus  d a workbook that should be bought by every parent wh I had this book fifty years ago, many arguments with could have been avoided. My problem was that I had no idea about how to tackle homework and projects, because they always seemed huge and daunting. Learning how to break big assignments into manageable parts and to set tangible goals would have done wonders for me. It took me decades to learn what Knaus can teach in minutes. Buy this book."

> —**Derek Paar, PhD**, professor in the department of psychology at Springfield College, MA

"Bill Knaus has created a very useful guide for students of any age who have struggled with procrastination, and want to be college and/or career ready. Looking back on my experience as a high school teacher, high school principal, and school district superintendent, it was rare for me to see students that did not toil, in one way or another, with procrastination. I can see that this book would have been a tremendous help for any student who has left the dreaded book report for the last day (probably night) of Christmas vacation. If this sounds like you, this book is for you."

> —**Keith R. Burke**, former school administrator, and consultant to the New Hampshire Department of Education and other school districts throughout New England

"*Overcoming Procrastination for Teens* shows how to build powerful mental skills and use self-organizing tools to succeed in college preparation classes, and later in college. Along with engaging examples of teens meeting tough challenges, each new chapter builds on the one that came before it to create a pyramid of knowledge for success. I strongly recommend it."

> —**Susan Tapper, EdD**, professor emeritus in health education at San Francisco State University, and instructor for the University of San Diego Extension Program for Teacher Education Credentialing

"In this engaging and highly accessible book, psychologist Bill Knaus masterfully lays out useful strategies for overcoming procrastination habits that often lead students to underperform and suffer needless stress. Using metaphors such as the *Frog*, and the *Spirit of Reason*, he artfully drives home valuable life lessons, and then provides numerous skill-building exercises for internalizing rational anti-procrastination thinking and acting. This is the only book of its kind. All students—from high school through graduate school—should place a copy in their backpacks and read it!"

> —**Elliot D. Cohen, PhD**, professor and chair in the department of humanities at Indian River State College, FL

"Hats off to Bill Knaus. *Overcoming Procrastination for Teens* is a veritable feast—a smorgasbord of practical, usable, and effective cognitive and behavioral strategies for the high schooler, the college student, and anyone, for that matter who wishes to eliminate procrastination and make their goals a reality. It feeds the needs of the student, his or her parent, and those practitioners, like myself, who are called upon to help those already starved for success because of procrastination. Bon Appetit!"

> —**Russell Grieger, PhD**, is a licensed clinical psychologist in private practice, an organizational consultant, and adjunct professor at the University of Virginia

"The most frustrating, hair-pulling moments for parents occur when their teenager avoids, delays, or stubbornly resists doing their homework or other responsibilities. In this brilliantly conceived book, Bill Knaus throws a lifeline to both parents and teens by explaining what psychological processes are operating behind the procrastination and indecision, and then provides dozens of straightforward tips and techniques to overcome this problem. This groundbreaking book should be on every family's bookshelf!"

> —**Barry Lubetkin, PhD, ABPP**, director and founder of the Institute for Behavior Therapy in New York City, NY

"Written in an easy-to-understand, conversational style, *Overcoming Procrastination for Teens* provides wise ideas for teens (and their parents) on defeating procrastination. The reader will find engaging examples, where teens learn from teens, and where metaphors and stories make key ideas memorable. Teens who try just a few of these methods, and give themselves half a chance, are likely to gain a lot."

> —**William L. Golden, PhD**, licensed psychologist with a private practice in New York City and Briarcliff Manor, NY; author of several books; and faculty member at Cornell Medical College

"Bill Knaus' narrative style not only presents essential information in a highly reader-friendly way, but will also help readers retain the important aspects of the material. What's more, his emphasis on encouraging active participation with a variety of concrete and clearly illustrated tasks will almost certainly engage and reward the reader. Simply put, a must-read (and do) for any college-bound student grappling with the challenges of procrastination. Indeed, I plan to use it in my practice with many adults in addition to my adolescent clients, college-bound or not!"

> —**Clifford N. Lazarus, PhD**, licensed psychologist, and cofounder and director at the Lazarus Institute for Multimodal CBT

"Dear college-bound teen—don't leave your future to chance. Prepare now for the challenging road ahead. Learn to reduce procrastination and optimize your successes with Bill Knaus' gift for boosting your effectiveness. When you get to college, you'll be glad you did."

> —**Deborah Steinberg, MSW**, psychotherapist, former supervisor and board member at the Albert Ellis Institute, mindfulness facilitator, and coauthor of *How to Stick to a Diet*

"Bill Knaus has worked his way into the world of procrastinator thinking, and nailed the solutions to the 'putting it off' mentality. His solution takes the young (and not so young) procrastinator by the hand and provides the tools to getting it done!"

> —**Joel Block, PhD, ABPP**, diplomate of the American Board of Professional Psychology, and assistant clinical professor of psychology and psychiatry at Hofstra Northwell School of Medicine

"In *Overcoming Procrastination for Teens*, Bill Knaus shows young people how to overcome a great barrier to using their talents effectively—themselves! I strongly recommend this research-grounded book not only to teen readers, but also to their parents and to the counselors who work with teens who struggle with procrastination."

> —**Mike Abrams, PhD, MBA, ABPP**, licensed psychologist, New York
>   University faculty member, psychotherapist supervisor at the Albert
>   Ellis Institute, and author and coauthor of four books

"In spite of our best intentions, we often do exactly the wrong thing at the expense of our future selves. Teenagers especially can benefit by learning to hack their tendencies towards inaction and distraction by understanding and applying Bill Knaus' lucid and practical approach."

> —**Nando Pelusi, PhD**, clinical psychologist, founding member of
>   Applied Evolutionary Psychology Society, and contributing editor for
>   *Psychology Today*

"Procrastination can profoundly affect a teen's life by contributing to poor grades, high dropout rates, and delayed graduation from college. Bill Knaus, the leading authority on the subject of procrastination, advances our understanding of how and why we often don't do what"s best for ourselves, and how to change for the better. Each chapter overflows with useful examples and practical suggestions for overcoming this vexing problem. Knaus' step-by-step prescriptions will greatly benefit any teen hoping to increase success in or out of school."

> —**Ronald Murphy, PhD**, practicing clinical psychologist for over forty
>   years, former professor at New York University, and supervisor of
>   graduate clinical trainees in the doctoral program in clinical psychology
>   at Teachers College of Columbia University

"*Overcoming Procrastination for Teens* is a must-read for those with acute or chronic procrastination. The book offers practical and useful evidence-based techniques and strategies to conquer a student's worst habit—procrastination. Not only is this a useful book for college-bound students, but also for health professionals—especially those who provide student counseling services."

> —**Sam Klarreich, PhD**, psychologist, author, advisor, senior-level consultant, and president of The Berkeley Centre for Effectiveness, and The Centre for Rational Emotive Therapy

"My most challenging encounters in facilitating over three thousand SMART Recovery meetings have been with groups of teens. Until I read Bill Knaus' current addition to his oeuvre, I was oblivious to how pervasive procrastination was in inhibiting teens from succeeding in their college studies or in stopping an addiction. Addressing procrastination using Knaus' pragmatic approach should go a long way towards avoiding the often-failed 'New Year's Resolution' approach to success. I'll happily add ideas from this book to what I do."

> —**Joe Gerstein, MD, FACP**, retired professor at Harvard Medical School, and founding president of SMART Recovery

"Teen procrastination is no match for the magic of psychologist Bill Knaus. His comprehensive study of this challenging problem has yielded a book that is chock-full of practical strategies that will move regular teens to become remarkable ones. He shares his innovative concepts through parables, metaphors, and stories that will reach even the hardcore procrastinating teen. If you work with teens, live with teens, or are a teen, this book is for you."

> —**Jon Carlson, PsyD, EdD, ABPP**, distinguished professor at Adler University in Chicago, IL

"Except, perhaps, for depression, nothing has killed more dreams and aspirations than procrastination. This present book is the glorious culmination of the journey Bill Knaus started decades ago to help people overcome procrastination. What could be better than putting both his new innovations and tried-and-true methods to work to beat procrastination in the teen years? The book is outstanding and I highly recommend it to not only teens but to everyone."

—**Sanjay Singh, MD, DNB, PhD**, professor of dermatology at the Institute of Medical Sciences, Banaras Hindu University, Varanasi, India

"Bravo! I am used to Bill Knaus hitting a home run with his books, but in his latest, *Overcoming Procrastination for Teens,* he knocked it out of the park! This leading authority on overcoming procrastination uses a unique storytelling approach to show how to navigate through one of the most difficult times in a teen's life. If you are a teen, or a parent of a teen, buy the book. It's an indispensable guide to academic success and beyond."

—**Vincent E. Parr, PhD**, clinical psychologist at the Institute for Rational Living ZRL in Tampa, FL

overcoming procrastination for teens

a cbt guide for college-bound students

WILLIAM J. KNAUS, EdD

Instant Help Books
An Imprint of New Harbinger Publications, Inc.

Publisher's Note

This publication is designed to provide accurate and authoritative information in regard to the subject matter covered. It is sold with the understanding that the publisher is not engaged in rendering psychological, financial, legal, or other professional services. If expert assistance or counseling is needed, the services of a competent professional should be sought.

Distributed in Canada by Raincoast Books

Copyright © 2016 by William J. Knaus
       Instant Help Books
       An imprint of New Harbinger Publications, Inc.
       5674 Shattuck Avenue
       Oakland, CA 94609
       www.newharbinger.com

Cover design by Amy Shoup

Acquired by Jess O'Brien

Edited by Gretel Hakanson

Library of Congress Cataloging-in-Publication Data on file

18   17   16

10   9   8   7   6   5   4   3   2   1   First Printing

Contents

Introduction

Learning to reduce procrastination may be the best thing you can do to prepare yourself for college. You'll build skills for success. You'll put yourself in control of improving your high school and college grades. You'll have fewer hassles. You can do this without taking time away from your friendships, social life, and fun things that you like to do. Indeed, you'll have more stress-free time to do what you like.

Procrastination: An Ongoing Challenge that You Can Meet

If you expect to overcome procrastination when you get to college, think again. College courses are demanding. More information will come your way, and it will come faster. You'll have a new, open schedule to manage. You'll have more distractions to control. You'll have to take a lion's share of responsibility for your own learning if you expect to succeed.

Given all the adjustments you'll need to make in college, it's not surprising that most of your peers will procrastinate more in college than they did in high school. When researchers surveyed college students about their most pressing problems, 60 percent said that procrastination topped their list.

Procrastination may be one of the most underrated reasons for academic problems in college. It can affect whether you graduate late from college or graduate at all. Here are some eye-opening numbers:

- Between 5 and 7.5 percent of community-college students complete full-time studies in two years, and between 38 and 42 percent finish within six years.

- On average, 35 percent of entering freshmen finish four-year bachelor's degrees in four years, and 59 percent finish in six years. (Graduation rates for the most selective schools are much higher.)

- Between 43 and 51 percent of doctoral students don't finish their degrees.

- In the United States, 31 million people who started college never finished.

Students graduate late from college for all sorts of reasons, but from what I can see, procrastination is among the top causes. Learn to overcome procrastination before you get to college and you'll avoid many needless hassles with studies and assignments both now and later. You'll improve your chances of graduating on time and of getting a good job or admission into a graduate school. You may develop a fondness for learning that will benefit you over a lifetime.

Self-Mastery: A Prime Solution to Procrastination

Over 2,500 years ago, people journeyed to the temple of the Oracle of Delphi to hear a priestess who prophesized and gave wise advice. As the temple visitors approached, they saw these two words carved on a temple stone: "Know Thyself." The path to knowing yourself is the path of self-discovery. Self-mastery is a big part of this process.

Self-mastery is a process with a purpose. You build a stronger, more efficient, and more effective *you* by developing skills for understanding yourself very well. You do this by acting to meet personal challenges and to solve tough problems. You make a special effort to persist even when you feel uncertain about what to do. You experiment, use feedback, and stretch your positive abilities. You won't be perfect. Who is? You'll make mistakes. Who doesn't?

In this book, you'll learn the following self-mastery skills:

- **Problem-solving.** As you hone your problem-solving ability, you earn confidence in your abilities.

- **Reflecting and reasoning.** You'll think more clearly and have fewer needless troubles.

- **Separating what is important from what is not.** By acting on what is important (priorities first), you avoid procrastination traps.

- **Monitoring and regulating your thoughts, emotions, and actions to produce superior results.** By taking this step, you put yourself on a path to knowledge and wisdom.

- **Building resilience by choosing to tough it out with your studies when there is no other meaningful alternative.** When you don't run from difficulty, you position yourself to master many worthy challenges.

- **Setting attainable goals, planning, organizing for success, and executing your plan effectively.** You take charge of yourself when following this direction.

- **Accepting obstacles and setbacks as part of the learning process.** That's what the inventor Thomas Edison did. Before he succeeded in creating a functional light bulb, he tried thousands of filaments that didn't work before he found one that did.

- **Learning to relax, mobilize, and then act effectively when you need peak performance.** You can create this tailwind at will.

- **Freeing yourself from the constraints of procrastination to enjoy your life more.**

What's your incentive to do better for yourself? Think about the things that procrastination is keeping you from doing. Keep those things in mind as you work though this book, and let the vision of the successful completion of them be the incentive you need to take charge of yourself and accomplish more.

The Do-It-Now Way

Knowing yourself by testing yourself is an effective way to build self-confidence and self-acceptance, and to strengthen your natural abilities to relate well with others. You can help yourself do these things by following a *do-it-now* philosophy for developing your finest positive qualities. The spirit of this philosophy flows through this book.

The idea behind this approach is to do reasonable things in a reasonable way in a reasonable time to increase your chances for health, happiness, and accomplishments. The "now" part of reasonable means starting as soon as feasible.

What is reasonable will vary by situation. Here is what "reasonable" means:

- Doing reasonable things refers to priorities, or the most pressing, timely, and important things that you have to do.

- Doing something in a reasonable time refers to timing and pacing yourself so you can be done on time and with less stress.

- Doing things in a reasonable way refers to doing the best you can with the resources you have available.

By making a reasonable effort to stay on this path, you are in a position to

- get important things done,

- achieve more in less time,

- learn what you are capable of doing,

- build a positive, fact-based self-concept, and

- run your life better.

It takes time and practice to build a do-it-now habit. After all, you've had years practicing procrastination. However, by making a good faith effort to follow the do-it-now way, you can make progress.

What to Expect

By taking a self-mastery approach, you can increase positive experiences by reducing the negatives that co-occur with procrastination. In each chapter, you'll find different self-mastery skills to develop and self-help experiments to try. These are no-failure experiments where you'll learn what works, what doesn't, and what you can do to continue to improve.

Some chapters in this book have stories about teens who learned to overcome procrastination obstacles with self-mastery efforts. Some feature metaphorical guides (such as a friendly frog) whose purpose is to help you discover your inner strengths and put them to good use. Ideas through stories are easier to remember than lists of concepts. These stories can help you recognize situations where the specific self-mastery skill described applies to you. The stories and metaphors also aid problem recognition. When you can anticipate a problem, you are in a good position to solve it.

We live in a blame culture where it is easier to find fault than correct errors. At the same time, positive peer support can make a big difference in your efforts to develop self-mastery skills. Thus, you'll find examples of like-minded teens who share a common cause to achieve self-mastery over procrastination and who are willing to share ideas with others.

Some ideas about procrastination may resonate with you more than others. For example, in chapter 1 you'll find a procrastination test to help you recognize procrastination situations that are important for you to overcome.

It's ironic that a procrastination habit takes work to correct. That is partially because procrastination is an impediment to correcting itself. However, you don't have to do it all at once or on your own.

This book is not a quick read like a novel. Take time to digest the ideas. Play with them—that's a good way of learning how to use them. Then read it again the summer before you go to college. You are likely to gain ground with each new reading.

Be realistic in your expectations. You won't be 100 percent successful in permanently eliminating procrastination. You don't need to be. In baseball, a 300 hitter gets six hits for every twenty times at bat. That's a very good average. A 350 hitter is a superstar. What's the difference? The 350 hitter gets one additional hit every twenty times at bat. Cumulatively, a small difference can make a big difference.

To use this book effectively, stretch a bit. Actively strive to boost your skills for persisting in both starting and finishing assignments. Work the experiments that apply to you. Record what happens—that technique supports progress. Use the worksheets that are available for many of the experiments, if you need to. (You can find them at http://www.newharbinger.com/34572.) Make yourself the executive of your destiny. You can do this! Then, take this book with you to college. I think you'll be glad that you did.

chapter 1

Procrastination's Web

Keep putting things off until another day and you'll find yourself on the strands of *procrastination's web*. This sticky spider web has many interconnecting strands that can be challenging to escape from once you're stuck.

Life is simpler off the web. So what can you do to get to that simpler place? You can free yourself from procrastination's sticky strands using the tools in this book. In this chapter, you'll see how to spot the different parts of a procrastination *process*. You'll see what you can do to get yourself off the web at any time or place.

What Is Procrastination?

Procrastination is an emotionally driven performance problem where time is an important factor. When you are procrastinating, you are both avoiding doing something uncomfortable or threatening and approaching something more pleasurable, stimulating, or less uncomfortable.

When you procrastinate, you needlessly (sometimes unconsciously) put off performing a timely and important activity until another day or time. This process starts with a perception and negative feeling about an activity or situation. Then, when you procrastinate, you *always* substitute something less relevant or less pressing. For example, you have a biology test tomorrow. Instead of studying, you text, shuffle papers, join friends at the mall, or bicker with your parents. These substitution activities are procrastination's most visible feature.

When you procrastinate, you'll practically always engage in procrastination thinking, such as, *I'll do it later.* You may give yourself excuses to justify delaying, such as, *I'm too tired.*

Finding Where You Stand:
Procrastination Awareness Survey

If you believe you could improve yourself if you had the right tools, you are a good candidate for the information in this book. You'll find many tested ways to build your self-mastery skills as you decrease procrastination.

Overcoming procrastination starts with an analysis of what goes on when you procrastinate. Below is a list of statements to help you identify your procrastination hot spots. For each statement, there are explanations and solutions in this book for developing self-mastery skills for successfully combatting procrastination.

Instructions: If the statement sounds like you, put a checkmark in the "Like Me" column. (Don't concern yourself about how many items you check. Most questions are variations of a few basic causes.)

The "Chapter for Corrective Actions" column lists chapters in this book where you'll find information on the self-mastery skills for each item.

Item	Like Me	Chapter for Corrective Actions
1. I keep falling behind on my studies.		1
2. I don't pay attention to what I do when I procrastinate.		1
3. I feel trapped by procrastination.		1
4. I tell myself I work better under pressure.		2
5. I have trouble starting on assignments.		2
6. I feel pressured to perform as time runs out.		2
7. I procrastinate often.		3
8. I often don't think things out.		3
9. I normally do better when I think things out.		3
10. I daydream a lot.		4
11. I plan to do better later.		4
12. I need to feel inspired to begin an assignment.		4
13. I'm often unprepared.		5
14. I start many things and finish few.		5
15. I feel anxious before taking tests.		5
16. I'm only as good as my successes.		6
17. I'm afraid of failing.		6

18. I get sidetracked from my studies.	6
19. I have trouble staying organized.	7
20. I'm not good at planning.	7
21. I'd do better if I worked harder.	7
22. I feel stressed by schoolwork.	8
23. I lack confidence in my abilities.	8
24. I need a boost to get started.	8
25. I need to feel certain before I risk acting.	9
26. I hesitate too often.	9
27. I often wait until it is too late.	9
28. I have more ability than I show.	10
29. I get distracted easily.	10
30. I could use help managing my time.	10
31. I don't feel prepared for college.	11
32. I lack a clear direction in life.	11
33. I'm not sure what I'll do for a career.	11
34. I wish I knew how to succeed.	12
35. I wish I could stop procrastinating.	12
36. I often don't believe in myself.	12

By isolating procrastination hotspots, like the above, you'll know what areas to target for change. After you've worked on combatting procrastination for six weeks, do the survey again. See where you've improved and where you have work to do. Thereafter, check your progress every three months. By monitoring your progress, you may feel motivated to keep improving.

Getting Off Procrastination's Web

When you sidestep your high priorities, you are on the strands of procrastination's web, and it is difficult to get back on track. Getting off the web is not impossible, though. It's important to know that the spider and the web need not grab your attention.

Let's see how Dawn did this. Dawn is a very bright young woman whose procrastination affects her grades, reducing her chances of getting into the college of her choice.

Experimenting with a Procrastination Log

To understand how Dawn got herself on procrastination's web, Dawn created a *procrastination log* and wrote down what she did when she put off studying for an upcoming history quiz. The log gave her information for creating a self-mastery plan and for getting off procrastination's web.

Create your own log alongside Dawn's example. Your situation may be different from Dawn's. However, the important thing to note is the process that you follow when you procrastinate.

Dawn's situation:	Your situation:
An upcoming history quiz	
Dawn's Procrastination Activity Log	**Your Procrastination Activity Log** *(Note: it may be longer or shorter than Dawn's.)*
1. After school was out, I phoned my friend Sally. We talked about the cute new guy in school. That conversation lasted about a half-hour.	1.
2. I told myself that I was too tired to concentrate.	2.
3. I texted Logan to say that I liked the new sound system he installed in his car. We texted for about an hour.	3.
4. I told myself I would start studying after supper.	4.
5. After supper, to get in the mood for studying, I watched TV.	5.

6. I decided to tidy up my bedroom— to make it a more pleasant place to study.	6.
7. I was missing some of my notes and worried that the information would be on the test. I felt frantic. I looked for the notes, and finally found them.	7.
8. I felt too flustered to study. Besides, it was too late. I set my alarm for 5:00 a.m. I planned to study at that time.	8.
9. When the alarm went off, I punched the snooze button. About a half-hour later, I started to study.	9.
10. I felt rushed as I read the chapter and then tried to study the notes.	10.
11. I took the test and got a C+.	11.
12. I told myself that if I had more time to study, I would have done better. I'll start earlier and work harder next time.	12.

Record, Plan, Assess: Three Steps to Breaking a Procrastination Habit

After recording her procrastination habits, Dawn was amazed by what she did to avoid studying for the quiz. Although she enjoyed communicating with her friends and watching TV, she didn't like the idea of sidetracking herself at the wrong time. She felt bothered that she wasn't truthful with herself when she told herself she'd start earlier, work harder, and do better next time. She had made the same promise to herself many times before, and nothing had changed.

Dawn recorded her corrective actions. Here is her self-mastery action plan.

- "To be truthful with myself." Dawn reasoned that if she valued truth, the place to start was with herself. Her procrastination log allowed her to see the facts about what she was doing (and not doing) to study for her quiz.

- "To mark a start time on the calendar and stick to it." The data from her log documented that she started too late to do an adequate job. She concluded that best way for her to prevent procrastination was to stop sidetracking and start earlier.

- "Make the penalty for delaying greater than relief from delaying." To reinforce her commitment, Dawn told her best friend that she'd dress for school one day in an outfit from the 1950s if she didn't start at the time that she designated. Starting earlier was a far easier thing to do than that.

For her next test, Dawn started studying before the deadline she set for herself. She prepared adequately and was satisfied with the grade she earned on her test.

Your Three-Step Self-Mastery Experiment

When you examine your procrastination log, what do you find? Record your findings here.

Write down your action plan ideas and changes you can and will make to build self-mastery skills by substituting productive actions for procrastination distractions.

Record what happened when you executed your plan.

Your Progress Report

You'll find a section like this at the end of each chapter. It's for recording what you learned and found useful. Write down what you learned from this chapter and what actions you plan to take, and then record what resulted from taking those actions and what you've learned by answering the following questions.

1. What three key ideas from this chapter struck you as most important to remember?

2. What three actions can you take to combat your target procrastination problem?

3. What resulted when you took these actions?

4. What did you learn from the actions?

5. Specifically, what would you do differently next time?

By doing these progress report exercises, you are interacting with the material in this book and taking an important step in developing self-mastery skills. This work serves as a reminder about what you succeeded at doing that you can do again.

chapter 2

Eight Actions to Combat Procrastination

In this chapter, we'll explore eight actions you can take to stay on track when it is important for you to finish an assignment, pass a test, or take personal initiative. Let's see how Logan did this.

Logan normally waited then rushed at the last minute to finish assignments. He rationalized: "I work better under pressure." In reality, he didn't work better under pressure. When he felt rushed, it took him longer to figure out problems. He often felt overwhelmed by too many things to do and too little time to do them. He decided that he needed to make a change. He began with an upcoming statistics assignment that he'd ordinarily delay as long as he could. He picked this assignment to test a new way of following through on tough assignments.

Logan started by thinking about his thinking when he felt stressed. His stress thoughts were of two types. The first was a language of delaying: *I can't think of this right now. I don't feel like doing it. I'll start the homework later. I'll wait until I'm inspired.* The second form of self-talk expressed his feeling of threat: *I can't do this. I'll fail. I'll be embarrassed.* To dodge the threats, he filled in time with diversionary activities, such as playing computer games, daydreaming, napping, texting, watching TV, working on installing a new sound system in his car, and so forth.

Four Positive Actions: The Language of Choice, Commitment, Challenge, and Change

To turn things around for himself, Logan experimented with a language of *choice, commitment, challenge, and change* approach. These are the four C's for positive actions.

Language of Choice

A choice means you have two or more options. Logan's choice was between procrastinating and performing productively. He compared the choices:

Procrastination Choice	Productive Choice
To start early and fade fast, or to start late and finish late or not at all.	To start at a reasonable time. To continue. To take planned breaks. To finish before the deadline.

Seeing that the productive choice fit with his goal for self-improvement made it easier for Logan to choose the productive path.

Follow along with Logan. Pick an upcoming assignment that you would normally put off. Write it in the box below.

What does your procrastination choice sound like? What does your productive choice sound like?

Procrastination Choice	Productive Choice

Language of Commitment

A *commitment* is a pledge, promise, or expressed intent. For example, if you tell yourself, "I'll start reading the history chapter at 3:00 p.m. today and continue until I finish," that commitment shows intent.

Once he made his productive choice, Logan moved forward with commitment language. He compared his procrastination self-talk (the excuses he gave for delaying) to his commitment self-talk for following through on his statistics homework assignment. Here is what he wrote.

Procrastination Language	Commitment Language
I can't think of this right now.	I'll take the necessary steps to start and finish the assignment. That is my commitment to myself.
I'll start the homework later.	I'll get this assignment started in the next five minutes. That is my commitment to myself.
I'll wait until I'm inspired.	I'll start without being inspired. That is my commitment to myself.

Once he laid out his procrastination self-talk in writing, it looked shallow to him. The commitment language represented where he wanted to be.

What do you tell yourself when you delay? What's your commitment to yourself? Fill in the blanks in the chart that follows and see.

Procrastination Language	Commitment Language

Language of Challenge

How you talk to yourself about a challenging situation will influence how you feel and what you'll do. Logan felt tense because he thought, *I can't do this. I'll look like a fool if I fail. I'll feel like a loser.* This type of threat thinking can propel procrastination.

The language of challenge is the mirror opposite of threat thinking. You may or may not like an assignment. Nevertheless, you convincingly talk to yourself as if you believe that it is within your power to meet challenges.

Logan's inner speech reflected the threat that he felt when he thought about doing his statistics assignment. As he did with his commitment experiment, Logan compared his threat language to his challenge language.

Threat Language	Challenge Language
I can't do this.	I can start and see how far I can get.
I'll look like a fool if I fail.	I can put time into the statistics assignment and see how well I can do.
I'll feel like a loser.	The outcome will tell me where my next challenge lies.

Logan saw the connection between threat thinking and holding himself back. He realized that he could change his thinking. That's what the ancient mariners did when they learned the world was round and not flat; falling off the surface of the earth was a myth grounded in incorrect information.

What do you tell yourself when you feel threatened by a challenging situation? What can you tell yourself to challenge yourself? Fill in the blanks and see.

Threat Language	Challenge Language

Languages of choice, commitment, and challenge set the stage for action, or change.

Language of Change

Change language is a series of self-instructions that outline the steps that you will take to pursue a chosen course of action, for example, "I'll do this first. I'll do this second." You use these self-instructions to guide what you do.

After practicing language of choice, challenge, and commitment thinking, Logan launched into action. He gave himself step-by-step instructions for finishing his statistics assignment.

Change Language Instructions	Change Language Outcome
"I will now go to my desk."	Went to desk.
"I will open my statistics book."	Opened book.
"I will now start reading the chapter."	Started reading and continued until finished.

Using your chosen task as your reference, give yourself action instructions. Carry them out and record your results in the table below.

Change Language Instructions	Change Language Outcome

Using the four C's for positive action, Logan finished his statistics assignment a day early with minimal stress.

Three Behavioral Action Strategies

Here are three action steps that many have found helpful in combatting procrastination: the to-do list, the bits-and-pieces approach, and the five-minute plan.

To-Do List Techniques

Students who create and use *to-do lists* tend to procrastinate less and get better grades. The list serves as a reminder and an organizing system. Let's look at three types of to-do lists: ranked, sequenced, and check-off.

Let's suppose that you have many things to do over the next twelve hours. Some things are routine. Some are things you want to do. Some are priority responsibilities that you feel pressed to do. To keep yourself organized, make a ranked list when it is important to focus on your priorities first.

When you do a *ranked to-do list*, you list your priority tasks in their order of importance. Concentrate on your number one task first. (Your first priority is your top A priority, which is both the most important and the most pressing item on your list.)

To use the ranked system, list your A priorities (currently top-drawer in importance) first and your B priorities (currently medium-drawer in importance) second. You keep bottom-drawer activities (C priorities) off the list. The C activities are normally distractions, but some might be useful as rewards for actions.

Here's one of Logan's to-do lists for his academic A and B priorities.

To-Do List	Priority
Study for chemistry exam	A
Finish statistics homework	A
Start gathering information for history essay	B

Now it's your turn to experiment with a ranked to-do list.

To-Do List	Priority

The *sequenced to-do list* is an easy way to organize your priorities according to where they fall in the day, or in what order they will be done. Here is an example of Logan's sequenced to-do list.

Sequenced To-Do List	Priority
Study for chemistry examination	A
Attend soccer team meeting	A
Conference with English teacher	A
Finish statistics homework	A
Start gathering information for history essay	B

Now it's your turn to experiment with a sequenced to-do list.

Sequenced To-Do List	Priority

A *check-off sheet to-do list* is like the ranked or sequenced list with one added step. You check off each item as you complete it. Seeing something done and checked off a list can feel rewarding.

Here is an example of Logan's check-off sheet to-do list.

Sequence of Steps: Chemistry Exam	Check When Completed
1. Review notes.	
2. Reread chapter.	
3. Call Jen (chemistry wiz friend) and ask her to explain what I don't understand.	
4. Especially focus on topics the teacher said would be on exam.	
5. Skim over notes and chapter in study hall before exam.	

It's your turn to try the check-off sheet to-do list.

Sequence of Steps: _____	Check When Completed

The Bits-and-Pieces Approach

You can break most tasks down using a *bits-and-pieces approach*. This is useful for more complex assignments, such as doing an essay or science experiment.

First, think about the different parts of the task. Start at a logical point, and then do the first bit and then the next piece. Taking it in small bits, one at a time, helps you maintain momentum.

You may have many pending tasks rather than one or two large, complex ones. The bits-and-pieces approach applies in these situations too. You pick one task and start there. Then you pick away at the others in their order of importance.

Next time you have a complex or intimidating assignment, or multiple things to do, write the first step in the box below. Once you have a place to start, the challenges may not seem so daunting.

```
                                                              
                                                              
                                                              
                                                              
```

The Five-Minute Plan

Do you sometimes have trouble getting started, but once you get going, you do fine? Try the *five-minute plan* to get started. Here is what you do: Commit to short, successive work intervals, say five minutes each. At the end of the five minutes, you decide whether you'll commit to another five minutes. You continue until you decide to stop.

When you are ready to quit, take a few added minutes to prepare for your next work session. It is easier to pick up where you left off if you have laid out the next step. This can be as simple as a note to yourself that says, "Start reading page 56 at 3:45 this afternoon."

The to-do list, the bits-and-pieces approach, and the five-minute plan are helpful ways get started and keep rolling on your studies. Try using them in combination and see how that works for you.

The Rewards Experiment

You have your rewards system backward when you do a pleasurable diversion before finishing an assignment. This is like paying yourself before you do a job. When it comes to your studies, that rarely works well. By flipping things around, you can use a diversion to reward yourself for efficiency. Here's an example of how:

1. The time has come to do a task.

2. You have the urge to drink a cup of coffee first (your diversion).

3. You silently give yourself a self-instruction: "Do the assignment. Then reward yourself with a cup of coffee."

4. You do the assignment.

5. You reward yourself with the cup of coffee.

By using diversions to reward productive actions, you increase your chances of preventing a procrastination cycle. Test this method and see. (I filled in the first row as an example.)

Procrastination Diversions	Reward for Activity
Reading newspaper	Reading newspaper for five minutes as a reward for doing assignment

Your Progress Report

1. What three key ideas in this chapter struck you as most important to remember?

2. What three actions can you take to combat your target procrastination problem?

3. What resulted when you took these actions?

4. What did you learn from the actions?

5. What would you do differently next time?

chapter 3

How to Stop Dodging Discomfort

In this chapter, we'll explore how to combat discomfort-dodging procrastination by taking a fantasy excursion to Amphibian Way and see how certain regions of your brain can stir procrastination urges and what you can do about it. This is the first of several stories, myths, and fables on specific self-mastery skills to help you recognize and correct procrastination patterns. Put yourself into the story. See if you can make the concepts work for you.

The Amphibian Way: Procrastination by Default

Tomorrow's test, a confusing math problem, an upcoming class presentation—all can feel emotionally uncomfortable. The next thing you know you are checking Facebook or tweeting—doing almost anything but hitting the books to do the assignment. By examining what is happening, you can gain clarity and use this knowledge to overcome a procrastination pattern.

Let's take a fantasy journey to powerful earlier regions of your brain that evolved from our amphibian ancestors. There you meet a frog. You introduce yourself and ask for the frog's take on procrastination—you've heard he's a pro. Frog is friendly, cooperative, and quick to respond: "You must be the person who lives in the executive suite. I'm glad you stopped by. I'm happy to share what I know— I'm kind of an expert, you know." (The executive suite is your "new brain," or prefrontal cortex. This is where your *executive abilities*—those for reasoning, analyzing, planning, organizing, predicting, judging, and adjusting—reside.)

Frog goes on: "Procrastination is about reactions. You feel a negative sensation when you have something to do that you feel uncomfortable doing. It doesn't take much to kick-start escaping from this tension. A whisper of negative affect will do. You can think of this as jumping for cover. It's as simple as that."

You realize that a reactive frog lacks foresight. You think to yourself, *Jumping for cover won't work when an assignment is due.*

It's Jack's problem too, and he's struggling with it. When he has something tedious or uncomfortable to do, Jack, like Frog, jumps away. For example, he loves playing beautiful music, but not as much as he prefers to avoid uncomfortable practice sessions. So, when the time came to practice, he jumped to the refrigerator and snacked. Then he jumped to the mall to see if there was anything new to see. If you asked why, Jack would say, "I don't know. It's something that comes over me."

Jack's is a case of simple *default procrastination*: he feels uncomfortable, so he does something different. This reaction may not be fully under Jack's control. The amygdala, an almond-shaped region of his brain, appears to be part of the brain circuitry of procrastination. The amygdala contains a parallel set of neurons (nerve cells that transmit nerve impulses) that carry information about pleasant and unpleasant events and assign positive and negative emotions to the events.

Let's say that you feel uncomfortable about a school assignment and feel positive about a diversion. Here is a theory that can explain what is happening: You get a temporary (specious) double reward by avoiding doing something unpleasant and doing something pleasant instead. Positive and negative amygdala signals intermingle and kick-start the opening phases of default procrastination.

Both Jack and you can blame the amygdala for default procrastination. But that won't solve the problem. You do have the choice of accepting discomfort and acting productively. Let's turn to using your executive resources to address this natural and temporary amphibian reaction.

PURRRRS: A Tool for Short-Circuiting Procrastination

PURRRRS is an executive tool for slowing down, figuring things out, and acting reflectively and effectively. Let's start with the meaning of the acronym:

Pause. When you have an urge to jump, stop and tune in to what's happening.

Use your resources. Find enough personal resources to resist the impulse to get sidetracked, and slow down enough to make a real choice.

Reflect. Ask yourself: What's happening? Who's in charge? Is it your executive, or is it Frog?

Reason. Ask yourself: What do you gain by delaying? What do you lose? Take a language-of-change approach, such as, "I'll walk back to my desk. I'll sit down and open the book."

Respond. Implement each step of your language-of-change plan. If necessary, push yourself to start.

Review and revise. You can improve on most plans. Review what you've learned and devise ways to improve your plan and your follow-through efforts.

Stabilize. Keep practicing and improving until PURRRRS is automatic in situations where this method applies—that is, when your frog wants you to leap away when it is wise to persist.

Here's Jack's PURRRRS program, which he uses to help himself practice music.

PURRRRS	Actions Taken
Pause: Tune into what is happening.	Jack put a green dot on his thumb to remind himself to wait before sidetracking.
Use resources to resist impulses.	Jack remembered to think about what he wanted to accomplish and agreed with himself that he would slow down and think things through.
Reflect: Figure out what is going on.	Jack thought about the purpose that a default-procrastination urge served: nothing of much value. He considered the purpose that practicing his guitar served: he builds a skill for playing beautiful music.
Reason and plan it out.	Jack mapped out what he was going to do: pull out sheet music, take guitar out of its case, go to his bedroom, and start strumming.
Respond by putting your plan into action.	Jack used a language-of-change technique, talked himself through the paces, and started practicing.
Review and revise: Make adjustments to improve results. When warranted, try another way.	Jack reviewed his plan to see what he could improve. He thought he would do better to schedule practice time for when nobody was around. He gave himself a reward after practice—he enjoyed a cup of coffee.
Stabilize: Keep practicing and improving these skills until they are automatic.	Jack chose to make practice a priority. By regularly executing the priority, he gained a two-for-one benefit. He felt in control of himself. And he started playing guitar in a band.

It's your turn to try a PURRRRS experiment and see what you can do for yourself.

Start with what you are putting off and write it here:

_____

PURRRRS	Actions Taken
Pause: Tune into what is happening.	
Use resources to resist impulses.	
Reflect: Figure out what is going on.	
Reason and plan it out.	
Respond by putting your plan into action.	
Review and revise: Make adjustments to improve results. When warranted, try another way.	
Stabilize: Keep practicing and improving these skills until they are automatic.	

Controlling Distractions

Distractions are part of life. You hear your cell phone ring. You see a bird in flight. As your attention switches from one thing to another, you engage different regions of your brain. Each switch takes a brief time for the brain to adjust. These changes take place beneath your level of awareness. This switching process is a normal part of daily life, too. However, switching can be a hindrance when you are trying to learn a complex subject and need to concentrate.

When you are doing a homework assignment, your flexible brain keeps adapting as you switch tasks. For example, you start studying physics. You pause to play a computer game. You start calculating. A friend calls. You go back to calculating. It takes time and energy for different brain regions to adjust when you switch tasks. Thus, when it comes to doing a hard assignment, you'll lose some efficiency by retracing some of your steps each time you switch tasks.

Switching between tasks also interferes with working memory. This memory is similar to random access memory (RAM) on a computer or SMS on a mobile phone. If you switch off the device, you lose the data. For example, if you get a phone call when memorizing a list, you are likely to retrace some of the steps that you have already taken after you finish the call. To save time and effort, you can avoid a switching effect by avoiding the distractions.

When you look to your future as a college student, here is something to consider about technical distractions: College students fall into the task-switching trap when listening to lectures while using technical devices. Most believe that they can multitask efficiently. Brain-scan research suggests that this belief is an illusion. They lose efficiency and are more likely to miss points and not do as well as others who don't distract themselves in this way.

You can't control what your brain does when you switch between tasks. However, you can reduce factors in your environment that create switching effects while you are studying. When you have a subject to study that takes a lot of concentration, you can minimize these distractions by putting yourself in a place where you can concentrate without interruptions.

Benefit Analysis: A Tool for Choosing Action over Procrastination

When it comes to overriding urges to procrastinate, perspective helps. A short- and long-term benefits analysis can help you avoid caving into procrastination urges. Let's use completing college applications as an example for comparing Frog's way and the do-it-now way.

	Short-Term Benefits	Long-Term Benefits
Default Procrastination (Frog's Way)	Immediate relief from avoiding doing something challenging or unpleasant. Results: Application stays undone. Eventual feelings of uneasiness and stress.	There are no visible long-term benefits; you risk unpleasant results, such as running out of time, rushing, feeling stressed out, and performing well below your ability.
Do It Now! (The Executive Way)	Start to fill out application forms. Results: Momentum—once you've started something, it is usually easier to continue. A sense of relief and engagement.	Finish and submit the applications. Results: Improve your chances of getting into the college of your choice. Less needless stress. More accomplishments.

It is your turn to experiment with your short- and long-term benefits analysis:

Write your default-procrastination challenge here: _____

	Short-Term Benefits	Long-Term Benefits
Default Procrastination (Frog's Way)		
Do It Now! (The Executive Way)		

When you compare short- and long-term benefits of default procrastination against do-it-now actions, what do you conclude? For example, when you delay feeling uncomfortable, you are likely to feel worse and rushed later. You lose touch with what you are capable of doing.

Write your conclusions below.

Now that you know how Frog works and what to watch for, you are in position to use your self-monitoring ability to track what is going on and to assert control over Frog urges when you need to.

Your Progress Report

1. What three key ideas in this chapter struck you as most important to remember?

2. What three actions can you take to combat your target procrastination problem?

3. What resulted when you took these actions?

4. What did you learn from the actions?

5. What would you do differently next time?

chapter 4

Pitting Reason Against Procrastination Thinking

Jill was the mistress of tomorrow. Practically everything she didn't want to do today, she promised herself that she'd do tomorrow. She daydreamed a lot, especially when she was in classes that she found challenging. Like Logan, she normally started late and rushed to meet deadlines. In frenzied last-minute rushes, Jill duplicated previous efforts, scurried to find lost materials, and made silly mistakes. In spite of this calamity, Jill got by on her raw ability. She got B grades. Then, she had a wake-up call from her brother, Carl.

At the end of his first year at college, Carl was on academic probation. He candidly told Jill that his courses were more demanding than he had anticipated. He put off doing his coursework for as long as he could. He busied himself with his new friends. He spent a lot of time at the student union and playing intramural sports. He partied. He thought he'd do better later, but continued gliding until he could no longer do so, and he landed hard. He didn't want her to follow the path he followed.

Carl's unusual confession got Jill's attention. Her plan had been to boost her grades starting in her junior year. Meanwhile, she planned to take it easy and enjoy her sophomore year. Now, she wasn't so sure.

In this chapter, we'll explore a complex form of procrastination, and you'll see how Jill uses reason to combat procrastination thinking, take charge of her school assignments, and improve her chances for getting into the college of her choice—and for succeeding once she gets there. We'll start with a story of Jill and the Spirit of Reason.

Harnessing the Spirit of Reason

The Spirit of Reason is a friendly entity who can appear in whatever human form it chooses.

One day Jill went to the library to get a few books on how to study. She was in for a surprise. Unbeknownst to Jill, she was about to meet the Spirit of Reason in the guise of a librarian.

Jill approached the librarian and asked where she might find the study skill books. "Ah," said the Spirit of Reason, "I was looking for similar answers many years ago. What would you like to know?"

In the brief discussion that followed, Reason quickly saw that Jill had both productive and procrastination beliefs. Her productive beliefs included (1) I can set useful goals, (2) I can take actions to achieve my goals, and (3) I can learn what I need to know to solve my problems. If you saw Jill following her productive beliefs, you'd have the impression that she was a happy, self-confident, achieving person.

Jill's procrastination beliefs painted another picture: (1) *I need to warm up to an assignment before I can do it*; (2) *if I have an urge to do something different, I can't resist it*; and (3) *I can only start as time is running out.* If you saw Jill following her procrastination beliefs, you'd have the impression that she was on a path to underachievement.

Reason explained it to Jill this way: "When you have two different views about the same situation, perhaps you can learn to judge which view is more likely to be true or to work better for you. To aid you in forming these judgments, here are a few things about procrastination thinking that are helpful to know.

"Procrastination thinking is self-talk that falsely justifies putting off a timely activity. You tell yourself that you are too tired, not in the mood, the activity is boring, you'll do better tomorrow or sometime later.

"The *tomorrow illusion* is the belief that you can always do tomorrow what you don't want to do today. However, you conveniently forget about negative repercussions. The singer Dean Martin captured this idea in the 'Mañana (Is Good Enough for Me)' song. In the *mañana* world, tomorrow is soon enough to fix a broken window to stop the rain from pouring in and to fix a car that needs a motor to go somewhere.

"The song suggests a casual attitude about procrastination. However, in the real world, there is an added cost of waiting to repair the roof. You'll have water damage in your house.

"Fool yourself with tomorrow thinking, and you live with false hopes. You may think that someday you'll fix what's broken. You may think the same way about schoolwork. When these fictions are part of your belief system, they become your reality in situations where they surface.

"How do you know which of your emotions and actions come from fictions? One place to start is to see where you repeat patterns that lead to the same poor results. Procrastination is one such pattern."

Jill said, "That sounds complicated. How do you do this?"

Reason said: "Let's do an experiment. You compare your productive and procrastination beliefs about an assignment, and you examine the results. What is the most pressing assignment that you are putting off?"

Jill said, "That's an easy one. I'm putting off an essay on *Macbeth*."

With Reason's help, Jill mapped out a comparison between three productive beliefs and three corresponding procrastination beliefs.

Productive Beliefs	Results	Procrastination Beliefs	Results
I can set productive goals.	A sense of direction.	I need more time to warm up to doing the essay.	Delays, stress, and fewer accomplishments.
I have the ability to operate self-sufficiently.	Actions motivated by this belief.	I have urges to delay that I can't resist.	By waiting to know everything, I sidetrack myself and rush at the end.
I can learn what I need to know to solve problems.	Solutions to problems.	I can only start when I have no better choice.	Half-hearted efforts to succeed.

When she saw her productive and procrastination beliefs and results side by side, it was easy for Jill to see the contradictions in her thinking. She had the ability to set goals, operate self-sufficiently, and solve problems. She also doubted her academic abilities. That was one of the causes for her procrastination. This led to a question to resolve a contradiction: If I have the ability to achieve, what is there to doubt about this ability?

Experimenting with Productive and Procrastination Beliefs

Pick an assignment that you are currently putting off. As you think about this assignment, list your top three productive and top three procrastination beliefs. Compare the results of each belief.

Productive Beliefs	Results	Procrastination Beliefs	Results

What did you learn from the experiment? How do you apply what you've learned? Write your answers below.

Challenging the Contradictions in Procrastination Thinking, Feelings, and Behaviors

Procrastination thinking is an excuse for not performing. You tell yourself, "I don't have time to study." Then you fritter the time you say you don't have by watching a sitcom on TV. You tell yourself that you are too tired to concentrate on solving a math problem. Then you play basketball with your friends. In these situations, what you say and what is true are contradictory. When you compare contrary views, it's harder to deceive yourself.

Here are three ways to challenge yourself to resolve contradictions: (1) the cognitive challenge, where you contradict procrastination thinking; (2) the emotive challenge, where you contradict thinking about procrastination-propelling emotions; and (3) the behavioral challenge, where you contradict thinking about diversionary actions.

This is Jill's experiment for challenging contradictions between reasoned and procrastination thinking.

Contradictions	Responses
Cognitive challenge: Jill believed she needed more time before she began, perhaps wait to warm to the idea of starting the essay. Her challenge was to change this view. *Cognitive action:* Ask pointed questions such as, "Where is the evidence that I will ever warm to this work?"	Jill worked on answering the question, and this is how she answered the cognitive part of this challenge: 1. I may never warm up to doing this essay. It is a hassle, and I know it. 2. If I want to get the essay off my back and get a credible grade, I had better accept that there is no easy way other than to start today. 3. I stopped conning myself into thinking that I would do better in the future.

Emotive challenge: Jill believed that if she felt an urge to avoid a homework assignment, she had no choice but to go along with the urge. Her challenge was to change his view. *Emotive action:* Measure how long the urge to delay lasts. Then jump into action whether you feel like doing it or not.	Jill worked on managing her tensions and procrastination urges, and this is what she found: 1. The urge to delay lasted about seven minutes. 2. I'm not afraid of the feeling of discomfort and can start whether or not I feel uncomfortable.
Behavioral challenge: Jill acted as if she believed that she could not start early to take steps toward productive goals. In short, it was too hard to start. *Behavioral action:* Open the book and start reading.	Jill focused on doing rather than stewing over starting the assignment, and this is what she found: 1. Despite what I told myself about the essay being too hard, I took a simple step in the direction of starting. 2. I can and did live through the tension of starting. 3. Once I started, I found it surprisingly easy to continue. 4. I can do tough things.

It's your turn to try a cognitive, emotive, and behavioral contradictions experiment.

The assignment or task that you are delaying: _____

Contradictions	Responses
Cognitive challenge: *Cognitive action:*	
Emotive challenge: *Emotive action:*	
Behavioral challenge: *Behavioral action:*	

Contingency Mañana Thinking and Procrastination

The *contingency mañana deception* is where you falsely make one action contingent on doing something else first. You'll do the assignment, but first you have to feel in the right mood. You'll write the essay, but first you have to think up a perfect opening statement. You decide to try out for the class play, but first you need to read books on acting.

Waiting to be in the right mood, waiting to think up a perfect opening line, and waiting to procure books are false contingencies. They distance you from what you are delaying. You don't need to meet any of them to start.

If you recognize the *contingency mañana deception* early in a procrastination cycle, you may be less inclined figuratively to tie your sneaker laces together and then wonder why you stumble.

Daydreaming and Fantasizing

Fantasy procrastination is daydreaming to avoid something you find unpleasant. Jill often daydreamed to escape schoolwork that she found unpleasant. As a result, she let a lot go until the last minute and felt overwhelmed by incomplete tasks.

She used a cognitive, emotive, and behavioral approach to lessen her fantasy procrastination. First, she identified the contradictions of her fantasy procrastination thinking and then used reason to disconfirm the fallacies in the fantasies.

Jill's Assignment: Chemistry Homework

Contradictions	Responses
Cognitive challenge: Jill acted as if it were safer to dream than to deal with a situation that she preferred to avoid. *Cognitive action*: Examine the purpose that fantasy procrastination serves.	Jill first worked on figuring out why she fantasized about success while she avoided taking the steps to success. This is what she found. Purposes served by fantasy procrastination: 1. I'm protecting myself from disappointment. 2. Fantasy helps me escape feeling insecure.
Emotive challenge: To manage feelings of anxieties and tensions during class time without fantasizing. *Emotive action*: Show myself I can handle tension.	Jill worked on accepting her anxieties and tensions as a temporary state. Jill needed to reason this out. She came up with three critical ideas about tolerating tension that radically changed her perspective on tension: 1. I have greater tension when I rush to finish what I delayed. I can function well when I'm under some tension. 2. I realize that choosing to experience tension is unappealing. Nevertheless, it is better than putting myself through an emotional wringer later. 3. I need to allow myself to live through the tension by putting myself through the paces of starting sooner rather than later.

| *Behavioral challenge*: To take productive steps that lead to positive outcomes.

Behavioral action: Convert problem awareness into problem-solving actions. | Here are Jill's action steps:

1. I focused on the steps I needed to take to complete a chemistry homework assignment.

2. I visualized taking the steps.

3. I took the steps I visualized taking.

4. I found that once I took the first few steps, the next steps became clear.

5. I finished the assignment before I expected to finish. |

It's your turn to try a contradictions experiment for when daydreaming and fantasizing get in the way of creating accomplishments.

The assignment or task that you are delaying: _____

Contradictions	Responses
Cognitive challenge: *Cognitive action:*	
Emotive challenge: *Emotive action:*	
Behavioral challenge: *Behavioral action:*	

Reason left a note for Jill in the book she borrowed that she referred to often and reminded her of her progress: "Translate reason into action and you'll procrastinate less."

Your Progress Report

1. What three key ideas in this chapter struck you as most important to remember?

2. What three actions can you take to combat your target procrastination problem?

3. What resulted when you took these actions?

4. What did you learn from the actions?

5. What would you do differently next time?

chapter 5

Getting Beyond Procrastination Obstacles

In this chapter, we'll look at how to strengthen three important self-mastery skills: preparing for success, following through without stopping mid-stream, and not letting test anxiety get the best of you. You'll meet three teens who met these challenges.

Setting the Groundwork for Success

In Aesop's fable *The Grasshopper and the Ants*, a grasshopper sang, danced, and fiddled the summer away. Meanwhile a colony of ants prepared for the winter. The summer ended. When the northern winds blew, a desperate grasshopper came to the ants for help.

Procrastination on preparation is as common today as when Aesop wrote this fable. This is putting off laying the groundwork for success. However, there is more. In academic settings, procrastination on preparation can have a double-whammy effect: (1) you fall behind when you don't prepare; (2) you risk a performance problem because you are not prepared. To turn things around, do what elite performers do to prepare themselves mentally and technically for performing at peak levels. Here are three mental preparations for achieving excellence:

1. **Failure proofing.** Errors and mistakes are necessary bumps on a long path to excelling. Elite performers focus on correcting, improving, playing through mistakes, and bouncing back smoothly. An elite athlete or musician anticipates doing well and behaves according to that belief. Consider the alternative. If you believe that you are fated to fail, you are likely to put things off or make half-hearted efforts. You might also pressure yourself to act to avoid failing. You are more likely to choke under this kind of pressure.

2. **Mental rehearsal.** The most proficient surgeons practice mentally before they start working. On average, they perform better and make fewer errors. Musicians and athletes who mentally rehearse typically do better than those who don't or won't. Consider the alternative. You wait and hope for the best. That rarely turns out well.

3. **Pace training.** It takes time and practice for your brain to develop mental networks for complex new learnings. Rushing a process that takes time is like throwing tomato soup into a microwave and expecting to take out excellent spaghetti sauce. By getting more precise on pacing, you develop the skill of estimating how long it takes to do most things, and then test your time estimate against your performance.

Let's look at how Ethan developed an elite-performer self-mastery skill. Throughout middle school, Ethan did as little as he could. In his first year of high school, the work was more demanding. He was unprepared for that. He started getting low grades. That was enough to cause him to think seriously about turning things around and doing better with his studies. Here is Ethan's self-mastery plan and the results from his six-week mental preparation experiment.

Self-Mastery	Plan	Results
Failure Proofing	View learning as playing through mistakes while studying to improve.	More efficiently followed through with studies.
Mental Rehearsal	Mentally break learning tasks down into parts. Imagine gathering materials. Imagine studying. Imagine making a good faith effort to figure out how to fill gaps in knowledge.	Improved skill in using mental preparation for engaging complex learning projects. I now do this automatically.
Pace Training	Execute the mentally rehearsed plan. Learn to pace myself to gain the most from the time and effort I put into learning.	Learned how to establish control over learning without trying to rush things through. I procrastinated less and my grades improved.

If you too would like to strengthen your preparation skills, here is a framework for your experiment in preparation.

Self-Mastery	Plan	Results
Failure Proofing		
Mental Rehearsal		
Pace Training		

Following Through Without Stopping Midstream

Behavioral procrastination is starting something that benefits you and then quitting before you finish. For example, you prepare for doing an assignment. You start working on the assignment. You stop midstream.

Olivia was painfully aware of behavioral procrastination. For example, items that she purchased for hobbies remained in their packaging. A tall pile of novels she bought to read gathered dust in the corner of her room. After she wrote her to-do lists, she put them aside and didn't use them.

Olivia followed the same pattern with her studies. She started strong then faded fast. Unlike the hobbies she hoped to do someday, she had deadlines to meet for her studies.

Olivia reviewed what happened when she started, stopped, and then rushed to finish a history essay on King George III and the American Revolution. She recalled that she set a time for studying. She started on time. She checked Internet resources. She read the assigned chapter in the text. While the information was fresh in her mind, she sidetracked herself by checking her smartphone and texting her friends. In fact, she distracted herself so much that she lost track of the distractions.

Olivia was comfortable with preparing herself to do most assignments. However, when it came to writing assignments, she started strong by gathering materials and procrastinated when the time came for writing.

Olivia found a description of behavioral procrastination in an old book titled *Do It Now: How to Stop Procrastinating. Wow,* she thought, *this sounds like me.* She thought about what she read and then asked herself three questions about when she stopped midstream. That effort paid off. The following shows the questions and the steps she took to break her behavioral procrastination cycles.

Question	Result	Action Plan	Six-Week Result
What happens just before I start behaviorally procrastinating?	I feel tense about the writing. I don't know what to say in my first paragraph.	Accept this feeling as a fleeting emotion that won't last forever. So what If I don't have a perfect opening statement. I'll start with one that is good enough and then revise it if I think of a better one.	By using this combination method, I felt in control. Over the past six weeks, I got increasingly better at finishing without stopping midstream.
What did I tell myself when I started behaviorally procrastinating?	I don't want to do this essay. I'll finish later when I feel inspired to write.	Accept that I don't have to want to do the essay. However, I do want a decent grade. Question the belief: Where is the evidence that I'll feel inspired to do this assignment later?	I can better focus my attention on solving problems. There is no evidence I'll feel inspired, but there is ample evidence that I'll feel pressured later.
What do I do when I behaviorally procrastinate?	I daydream. I snack.	Instead of daydreaming or snacking, execute a ready-ser-go technique: To get ready, take a two-minute break. That's the ready part. Mentally rehearse the steps that I'll follow next. That's the set part. Use the five-minute plan to start again. That's the go part.	I can assert control over what I do. I daydream less. By learning to live with the initial tension about writing, I found that procrastination did not get out of control.

If you behaviorally procrastinate, what's your six-week experiment to break this habit?

Question	Result	Action Plan	Six-Week Result
What happens just before I start behaviorally procrastinating?			
What did I tell myself when I started behaviorally procrastinating?			
What do I do when I behaviorally procrastinate?			

Don't Let Test Anxiety Get the Best of You

Test anxiety is common among high school and college students. Mild or moderate test anxiety will probably not affect a test score, providing you don't procrastinate on studying. High anxiety may not affect the results if the test is easy. However, excess worry and distress might spur procrastinating, and this can result in a lower grade, especially for tests where preparation takes concentration.

Test anxiety is about the future. You feel vulnerable and threatened now because you don't think you will be able to cope effectively later. The most direct way to overcome test anxiety is to practice taking tests until they become routine. However, what do you do when you are stuck on procrastination's web along the way?

Luis's chemistry midterm was coming up in a week. He worried that he couldn't understand the subject well enough to pass the test. He worried about failing. He dreaded feeling anxious and spacing out during the test. He dreaded that his anxiety would wreck his performance. To escape anxiety, he procrastinated by playing Sim City. Then he sketched motorcycles on his artist's pad. He wanted to wait to feel relaxed before studying. This was an example of test anxiety that interfered with preparation. It was also an example of procrastination on learning ways to cope with text anxiety.

Since Luis's test anxiety was about a future chemistry test, he had time to figure out how to cope effectively. He got some help from his friend Lloyd, who suggested that Luis gather information about procrastinating. He heard that combination procrastination was very common (procrastinating in different ways and for different reasons to avoid the same thing).

Luis thought about what Lloyd said about the different forms that procrastination takes. He then read several *Psychology Today* blogs on procrastination authored by Bill Knaus, EdD. That helped him pin down three procrastination obstacles that fit with his experiences: thinking procrastination, secondary procrastination, and reactance procrastination. Here is what Luis did to stop procrastinating on overcoming his chemistry test anxiety.

Procrastination Barriers	Action Plan	Results of Action Taken
Thinking procrastination is putting off the mental work of solving challenging problems.	Compare belief that I can't understand chemistry with my previous class performances and test results that show I can learn chemistry. Talk it out with my friend Jill, an expert on using reason against procrastination thinking.	Looked at the facts. Showed myself that I knew enough in the past to pass chemistry tests. Felt hopeful. Jill pointed out that by refusing to allow a grade to define me, I failure-proof myself. Jill suggested that I tune into what I'm thinking while I'm avoiding an academic threat. One thought stood out. I believed it was impossible for me to take a test without feeling anxious. I realized that I have taken some tests without feeling anxious. Therefore, it is possible for me to take the chemistry test without dread.

Procrastination Barriers	Action Plan	Results of Action Taken
Secondary procrastination is putting something off because you feel anxious, stressed, or in a down mood. The problem is twofold: (1) You procrastinate on dealing with the distress emotion, and (2) you put things off until you feel in control, which might not happen soon.	Allow myself to start studying without a precondition of feeling relaxed first.	Worked on secondary anxiety by facing what I feared.
	Clear aside area for study.	Accomplished
	Skim material.	Accomplished
	Work on what I had confidence that I could do.	Accomplished
	Where I have trouble understanding a point, view YouTube presentations on what I am studying.	Found that different views on the same subject helped me understand the material that will be on the test.
	In the next two days, take eight sample chemistry tests that cover the same area that my upcoming chemistry test will cover.	Practice tests helped ease tension about taking tests.
	Instead of using Sim City as a distraction from anxiety, use Sim City as a reward for studying.	This gave me something to look forward to doing. A nice added incentive!

Procrastination Barriers	Action Plan	Results of Action Taken
Reactance procrastination is putting off doing a timely and relevant activity because you believe it interferes with privileges and freedoms, such as playing a computer game or pursuing a sketching hobby.	Explore how doing a school assignment is a challenge to my sense of freedom and autonomy.	I gain little by making a school assignment into an autonomy contest. I give the teachers what they want, which is a good performance on my part, and I get what I want, which is positive recognition and higher grades. Realized that procrastination deprives me of the freedom of exercising self-control. By keeping these two ideas in mind, I discovered a sense of discipline and control that I thought I lacked.

When you are anxious about a performance (such as a test, playing a sport, singing before a group), and if Luis's solution resonates with you, consider combatting thinking procrastination, secondary procrastination, reactance procrastination, or whatever other form of procrastination that gets you stuck on procrastination's web. Here is a framework for you to deal with your combination of procrastination challenges, such as default procrastination, deadline procrastination, or any other types of procrastination that interfere with positive learning goals.

Procrastination Barriers	Action Plan	Results of Actions Taken

Your Progress Report

1. What three key ideas in this chapter struck you as most important to remember?

2. What three actions can you take to combat your target procrastination problem?

3. What resulted when you took these actions?

4. What did you learn from the actions?

5. What would you do differently next time?

chapter 6

Combatting Procrastination with Wisdom

In this chapter, you'll learn how to build academic self-confidence and lower your risk for procrastinating. To learn more, follow along with Jen.

Jen had a B- average. That was not good enough for her. She believed that unless she was an A student, she was a loser. At the same time, she doubted her abilities. She second-guessed herself a lot, hesitated, and procrastinated.

Jen worried about failing. She worried about what her peers and teachers thought of her. She worried about worrying. To block out her doubts and worries, she distracted herself. She'd stop at the mall daily on her way home from school. She'd look at new outfits. She'd scout out the office supply store for materials to improve her efficiency. When she got home, she actively engaged in busy work. She updated her Facebook page. She tidied up her overly clean bedroom. She puttered. She ran short on time. However, when she started studying, she worked conscientiously. If her performance dropped below her expectations, she sugarcoated the result by telling herself she could have done better if she'd had more time. She described her situation in this way: "I feel like my pet hamster when it's on a running wheel."

Jen had a strong incentive to get off the wheel. The spirit of wisdom had an answer.

Taking a Fantasy Journey with the Spirit of Wisdom

The Greek goddess Athena came to life full-grown and endowed with wisdom. For the rest of us, we gain wisdom through the hard knocks of wading through the ambiguities of life to gain clarity and knowledge.

The *Oxford Unabridged Dictionary* defines wisdom as the capacity to judge rightly on the matters of life. However, wisdom is richer, deeper, and broader than is described by this standard dictionary definition. And wisdom is not restricted to people with white hair. Actually, your teen years are a natural time to meet challenging life problems, and this is a good time to learn wise ways of operating.

Let's take a fantasy journey where a kindly spirit of Wisdom saw Jen's desperate situation. Rather than make a direct appearance, the spirit created clues for Jen to learn about herself, to appreciate herself, and to get off the running wheel.

Wisdom put an article in a success magazine in the office supply store. Listed on the cover, the magazine had an article titled "Getting Off the Running Wheel." Jen saw it. *Hmm*, she thought, *that sounds like me*. She looked at the article. It had five passages that attracted her attention. The first passage was titled "Reflections on Self-Doubt."

At times, Jen believed that she was not smart enough, brave enough, or talented enough to master a tough subject well enough. She tended to get down on herself, and she felt less confident. That was a vicious circle. The first passage gave Jen a way to scrap her self-critical view by exploring a self-accepting view.

The first passage said, "People who judge themselves harshly about their performances are often accepting of a friend's errors and mistakes and are quick to point out to the friend that perfect performances are not required for friendship. Would you think less well of a friend if that friend got a D grade in algebra? We appreciate friends for what they bring to a friendship. Is it possible to treat yourself like a friend?"

After reading the passage, Jen realized that she didn't apply the same standards to her friends that she applied to herself. At that moment, she began to doubt her belief that her worth and friendships depended on her grades.

The second passage was titled "Understanding the Variable Self." It said, "A *contingency-worth* belief is that your human worth depends on your performances. As a core belief, you may compare yourself to others and feel unworthy if someone does better than you in a subject, an athletic competition, or in a debate. Your beliefs about your academic abilities may vary by subject or by teacher. Your beliefs about your popularity may differ when you are among friends and when you are among strangers. A changing mood may affect what you believe about yourself or other people."

Jen could see that she was the one who gave herself a self-worth report card, and that report varied by subject and teacher. Clearly, with that kind of variability, she could not be only one way. She concluded that she'd wisely work to maintain her top grades and work to improve her other grades. Those report cards were measures of her performances. They were not a measure of herself.

When she flipped the page, she saw a passage titled "Changing a Dichotomous View." She read, "The founder of rational emotive therapy, Albert Ellis, noted that if you think in absolutes about yourself (good or bad, a winner or a loser), you restrict your intellectual freedom. That is because you are neither one thing, such as worthy, nor another, such as unworthy. The poet Walt Whitman earlier echoed this same idea when he described himself as 'contain[ing] multitudes.'"

Jen was a wiz in chemistry. She struggled with English. Did she judge her worth on her chemistry or her English grade?

Jen understood that she was multitudinous and had the ability to improve. She accepted that performances are measurable, even if people aren't. Her admission into a good college would depend on her academic performance. Her worth as a person would not.

Jen wondered what she could do to assert more control over her studies. When she came to the fourth passage, "Building Self-Efficacy," she flipped the page and discovered how.

She read, "Self-efficacy is a belief that you can organize, regulate, and direct your actions to master difficult challenges and improve. This is one of the more researched areas in psychology. Here is one result: Students with high self-efficacy beliefs tend to perform well in their studies. They focus on what to do and how to go about doing it. They manage their time well. Students with low self-efficacy beliefs generally have lower aspirations for success, don't rebound well from setbacks, pay too much attention to what they lack, procrastinate more, and normally do worse in their studies than they could capably do. Improving school performance by exchanging a low for a high self-efficacy belief seems like a simple thing to do. However, what is simple isn't necessarily easy to translate into practice."

To Jen, the self-efficacy idea sounded great. However, she wondered, *How does a self-efficacy belief translate into action?*

Jen flipped the next page and found the fifth passage, "Experimenting and Experiencing," which contained a four-point framework for transforming a self-efficacy belief into action.

She read, "You'll rarely develop wisdom by reading about wisdom, but rather you can develop wisdom by experimenting with concepts, such as self-efficacy, and learning what you can do and where you have limitations. Here is a framework for strengthening a self-efficacy belief.

1. Know what you want to accomplish.

2. Keep your attention on the process.

3. Identify procrastination obstacles before they take hold.

4. Give credibility to your self-efficacy belief through persisting."

The article had a self-efficacy experiment that Jen thought was just right for her. Here is how she completed it.

Self-Mastery Approach	Jen's Prescription
Know what you want to accomplish.	To build a strong self-efficacy belief. To reduce self-doubt. To substitute productive actions for diversions.
Keep your attention on the process.	What counts is the process, which is what you are doing to get to where you want to go. Organize, regulate, and direct yourself to build confidence in your competencies. Break skill down into workable parts. Progress comes in steps: When people try to change, they normally don't reach their goal on the first try. Ask for help when you have trouble understanding.
Combat procrastination obstacles.	Keep focused on the steps in the process. Mobilize personal resources for overcoming procrastination obstacles (such as tolerating and accepting tension and uncertainty as a natural part of life and using the five-minute plan).
Persist.	Believe that you can carry through with a constructive plan to achieve positive results. Practice persisting until it is a habit.

Jen turned a self-efficacy belief into action steps for improving her school performances.

It's your turn to experiment with applying a self-efficacy belief to an assignment using the following four-point framework.

Self-Mastery Approach	Your Prescription
Know what you want to accomplish.	
Keep your attention on the process.	
Combat procrastination obstacles.	
Persist.	

Given the choice, most reasonable people would choose to become wiser. Here are a few general guidelines on wisdom for those who choose this path:

- Wisdom is a byproduct of testing and inventing knowledge. This includes voluntarily initiating and applying knowledge, experience, and insight to solve problems with practical relevance to yourself and others.

- Wisdom reflects a realistic sense of awareness and perspective. Although wise thoughts reflect common sense views, wise ideas are ethereal (up in the clouds) unless put to good use.

- Wisdom reflects rational thinking that promotes health, happiness, and accomplishment. There are many ways to develop this power of thought, and one is to work at recognizing and stripping fictions and fallacies from your thinking. For example, a belief that you'll grow out of procrastination when you get to college is contrary to experience.

In the next chapter, you'll learn how to turn a self-efficacy belief into action by following a wise path of self-regulated learning.

Your Progress Report

1. What three key ideas in this chapter struck you as most important to remember?

2. What three actions can you take to combat your target procrastination problem?

3. What resulted when you took these actions?

4. What did you learn from the actions?

5. What would you do differently next time?

chapter 7

Using Your Executive Skills Effectively

In this chapter, you'll see how to take charge of your learning by setting goals that you can meet, staying on track, and performing well. Master this *self-regulated learning* skill before you get to college and you improve your chances for making life easier for yourself when you get there. To learn more, follow along with Molly. See how she applied this executive process to an online college course.

If you asked Molly about her grades—especially her math grades—you'd see a frown. She knew she could do better. So, what was going on? When it came to her studies, Molly spent a lot of time on procrastination's web. Let's start with Molly's incentive for getting off the web.

Since she was a child, Molly wanted to be a veterinarian. As soon as she was old enough, she did volunteer work at a nearby animal shelter. However, to study at a veterinary college, she'd have to perform at a high level at both high school and college. She wasn't doing that well in high school, and a large part of her academic problems was the result of a unique form of procrastinating. She prioritized organizing activities for her friends, such as hikes, parties, and civic projects, over her studies.

From talking with her college-bound friends, Molly understood that unless she improved her grades, her chances of going to a competitive college didn't look good. Her friend, Luis, said he read that top colleges favor students with four years of math. He suggested that she take an online math course at a local community college over the summer.

Molly knew she needed to make a change. She brought her parents and math teacher into the conversation. They liked the idea of the online course. They discussed practicing self-paced learning. This is a process where she would learn the material at a pace that she could manage. Self-paced learning had a practical value. As more and more college courses are now online, Molly knew she would be ahead of the game if she developed that self-mastery skill before she got to college. She picked a course that she and her math teacher thought that she could do. Her teacher told her to e-mail questions about math problems that she had difficulty solving.

Self-paced learning appealed to her. She told herself, "I can do this." Molly enrolled in the course.

The following experiment combines a self-regulated learning approach (which means you are in charge of your own learning) with a fable that delivers step-by-step instructions for how to do it. Here are four questions for you to keep in mind as you read the fable: (1) Does the fable help you remember the problem-solving approach and make it more accessible for use? (2) Do you improve on pacing your learning? (3) Does using a self-regulated learning approach help improve your learning performances? (4) Are you better prepared to recognize how procrastination can interfere with self-regulated learning and how to prevent this from happening?

A strange thing happened when Molly organized a hike and accidently went to the trail one day early. *Where is everyone?* she thought. Realizing her mistake, she decided to make the most of it. She saw an inviting new path and started to explore it. She thought, *If it's a neat way to go, I'll take my friends on it tomorrow.*

As she neared the trail, Molly saw an eagle on a high ledge. She heard a friendly voice coming from its direction. "Hi Molly. I'm from an ancient order of guides. From afar, I saw your plight. Can I help?" The eagle sounded wise.

Molly confided that she was worried about taking an online course in math. She explained that she wasn't good at math. She put off her math assignments more than any other subject. She wanted to try a different way and see if she could get college credit in her worst subject.

Eagle inquired, "Molly, what would you like to accomplish?"

Molly answered, "A B grade to support my college applications."

Eagle asked, "Molly, what is your plan for doing well in this course?

Molly answered, "I'll work harder."

Eagle asked, "Have you previously promised yourself that you would work harder on a subject?"

Molly answered, "Yes, many times."

Eagle lifted its wings said, "People who promise themselves that they'll work harder later often continue doing as they did before. Those who work to correct mistakes learn more and get more things done on time. Molly, when you organize events for your friends, you are exceptionally efficient. You have a natural knack for doing that. You can use this ability for how you go about learning math."

With that in mind, Molly said, "That sounds good to me. Let's go."

Then Eagle flew down, landed beside her, and began to explain how Molly could apply the five executive skills to the math course and to other things as well. She could use these skills to pace herself, procrastinate less, improve her academic performance, and prepare for college.

As Molly looked on, Eagle showed her a map of the executive path and said, "You'll find five markers on this trail. Each marker represents a skill that high-level executives use to create and to meet productive goals. You can apply these skills to learning and schoolwork. They also apply to organizing activities and to meeting personal challenges, such as meeting and overcoming procrastination obstacles."

Eagle said, "The first marker is *set a direction*. After that, you will come to *prepare an action plan*. The third marker is *organize for action*. After that, you will find *implement your plan*. The last marker is *review and revise*.

"This path winds and twists, and is rough and smooth at different times. You'll sometimes come to obstacles. You'll find branches to and from the procrastination trail. However, this is a far straighter, challenging, and more interesting path than the path of procrastination will ever be. Follow it and see where it leads. To help you find your way, I've left notes at each marker."

Then Eagle soared as high as it needed to go, but was never far away.

1. Set a Direction

As she started on the executive trail, Molly found Eagle's notes on goals at the *set a direction* marker:

"Some goals are vague, such as 'do great in math' or 'work harder' on homework assignments. They sound good but mean little. A workable goal breaks out into three main elements. It's meaningful, measurable, and attainable. Here is an example of a clearly stated short-term goal: *sign up for online math course by Wednesday*. Here is a longer-term goal: *master the content of a math course*. You can also add a performance goal, such as *attain a B or better grade*.

"Because it is consistent with what you want to accomplish, a goal of mastering the content of a math course is meaningful. It is measurable. That means that you can track your progress and see if you are on pace. If it is within your ability to accomplish, it is achievable. However, there is a Goldilocks factor. Like Goldilocks's porridge, strive to set goals that are neither too lofty nor unchallenging, rather just about right. Stretch a bit if you are not sure.

"Study goals typically fall into two major, sometimes overlapping, groups: mastery and performance goals. *Mastery goals* are for developing a skill, increasing your knowledge, or self-improving. When you feel motivated to master a subject, you'll normally feel more relaxed and absorbed in what you do. You'll tend to persist.

"Here is a mastery goal example: *to know how to solve advanced algebra problems to where you can instruct others to do the same.* That goal is meaningful. You can measure your progress. The knowledge is attainable. The danger with mastery goals is spending too much time learning one subject to the detriment of others. Keep track of where you are at in managing your other priorities and you are likely to avoid this trap.

"Practically all top performers (and successful organizations) have *performance goals*. A performance goal is a statement of your expected level of accomplishment. For example, Molly, you want to get a B or better average in math to support your college application. The danger with performance goals is in making your self-worth the same as your math score."

Molly started by setting both mastery and performance goals for the math course. That combination felt right to her. She identified an obstacle (procrastination) on the path. To overcome this obstacle, she set goals for overcoming procrastination. Here are Molly's goals:

Mastery Goal	Performance Goal	Goal for Overcoming Procrastination Obstacles
To learn the material in the math course to the point of mastery where I can help others with math.	To pass the course with a B grade.	Persisting without procrastinating by studying three hours a day (1.5 hours reading chapter materials and 1.5 hours solving math problems).

Molly was interested in helping others. By adding, "helping others" to her mastery goal, she gave herself an added incentive to learn.

What are your mastery and performance goals to support meeting an academic challenge? What are your goals for overcoming your procrastination obstacle(s)? Outline them below.

Mastery Goal	Performance Goal	Goal for Overcoming Procrastination Obstacles

By setting a direction and clarifying your goals, you put yourself on the executive trail. By recognizing your obstacle(s), you put yourself in a position to address them.

2. Prepare an Action Plan

At the second marker, Molly found Eagle's notes on action planning: "An action plan is a series of activities for how you'll achieve your goal(s). It answers the following questions: What do I do first? What do I do second? What do I do third?"

Molly had two planning experiments to perform. The first was to outline what she'd do to meet her mastery and performance goals. The second was to strip away procrastination barriers to avoid sabotaging her other two goals.

In making a study plan, Molly drew from her executive skill for social planning. You'll see her plan in the space below. In the space beside Molly's action plan, outline your plan for meeting your most pressing learning challenge.

Molly's Action Plan	Your Action Plan
Each day, Monday through Friday, watch online course video lecture.	
Study chapter.	
Work on problems.	
Get help when I hit a wall with a problem.	
Study for quiz.	
Take quiz.	
For final exam, review, do sample tests, and take the final exam.	

On the path to finishing her math course, Molly expected to meet her old nemesis, procrastination. Eagle flew down to help Molly devise a cognitive, emotive, and behavioral plan for combatting procrastination. This action plan consisted of four phases. The first was to outline her procrastination plan: what she would ordinarily do when she procrastinated. The second was to map cognitive, emotive, and behavior action plans. The third was to compare the plans. That comparison showed the fallacies in her procrastination approach. The comparison inspired her to stay away from procrastination's web.

Topic	Cognitive	Emotive	Behavioral
Procrastination Plan	I'll finish on time next time.	Relief from making a decision.	Repeat pattern of delay.
Action Plan	Instead of allowing myself to swallow false hope, I'll ask myself, "Looking at my history, where is the evidence that I'll do better later?" I'll remind myself of what really happens—I just keep repeating the same procrastination pattern. I'll guide myself through the paces by taking corrective actions. Here is a slogan I'll put on my computer: "Later is not good enough!"	Instead of running from anxiety, accept this feeling as temporary—like a passing wind, don't resist the flow. (Note: acceptance of tension often diminishes tension.)	Map procrastination to identify trouble spots, and then: Challenge myself by taking corrective actions to stay away from procrastination temptations. Commit to five minutes to start my study routine. If I can't figure out an assignment, I'll go back and review the video. If I still can't figure it out, I'll talk to math whiz friends, e-mail my math teacher, or talk with my parents about how to solve the problem(s).

It's your turn to create an action plan to get past a procrastination obstacle that you anticipate facing.

Topic	Cognitive	Emotive	Behavioral
Procrastination Plan			
Action Plan			

3. Organize for Action

When Molly got to the third marker, she found notes on organizing: "Organizing systems can save time and effort, and simplify your life. Scheduling is a way to organize your time to manage recurring activities. Here your challenge is to avoid procrastinating on setting and following your schedule."

Molly did her best work early in the day. She created a schedule where she could do math early. She also knew that she'd need to spend extra time on math—much more than she would ordinarily do. She committed herself to do whatever it took to do well in her course. Here is a schedule that she thought she would follow.

Monday Through Friday	Activity
7:30–7:50 a.m.	Review what I learned the previous day.
8:00–9:00 a.m.	Watch one-hour math lecture on computer.
9:00–10:30 a.m.	Study assigned chapter materials.
10:30 a.m.–12:00 p.m.	Work on assigned problems.
1:00–4:00 p.m.	Animal shelter for volunteer work.
4:00 p.m.	Spend time with friends.

It's your turn to organize to achieve your learning goal(s).

Monday Through Friday	Activity

4. Implement Your Plan

At the next marker, Molly found notes on implementing: "Implementation is the action stage where you move your plan forward through a series of actions."

Your executive skills apply to this process. They provide a structure for crossing a bridge between what you know about math now and what you'll know once you've reached the other side. The steps you take to cross this bridge of learning represent the efforts you make to acquire more knowledge about math.

Part of taking the executive path involves keeping track of what you are doing as you are doing it. Molly created a checklist and printed copies to cover the first five days of the math course. Her list reminded her what she was going to do. As she checked off the items, she felt a sense of accomplishment. When she made an improvement in her weekly plan, she revised and reprinted her checklist.

Molly's Routine Checklist	Molly's Checkmark
Use the five-minute plan to get started.	✓
Review what I learned the previous day.	✓
Watch one-hour math lecture on computer.	✓
Study the assigned chapter materials for the next 1.5 hours.	✓
Work on assigned problems for the next 1.5 hours.	✓
As needed, network with knowledgeable people about math problems I have trouble solving.	✓
As needed, combat procrastination urges as they arise.	✓

Create your own executive checklist for your project and check off each phase as you finish.

Your Routine Checklist	Your Checkmark

5. Review and Revise

Molly moved ahead and found Eagle's note on how to review and revise a self-regulation process:

"Self-feedback gives you at least two forms of useful information: (1) You have a check on yourself for how closely you stuck with your executive system. If you veered off track, you are in a position to make a knowledgeable revision and get back on course. (2) If you directly followed the executive self-regulated learning approach, you can directly measure the usefulness of your plan against its results and use this information to improve the process."

Molly mapped what she did in goal setting, planning, organizing, and implementing a self-regulated learning process. She noted the adjustments that she made to improve her performances.

Self-Regulation Technique	Goal Setting	Planning	Organizing	Implementing
Process	I set meaningful, measurable, and attainable goals.	I made plans that were consistent with the goals.	I scheduled time for routine activities.	I followed the plan with reasonable consistency.
Evaluation	The goals gave me something to shoot for. I had a sense of direction. I felt in control.	My plan was simple to follow.	1. The schedule I set simplified my day. 2. Twenty minutes was adequate to recheck the problems I did the previous day. My time estimation was on the mark. 3. Reading chapter text materials averaged out to an hour and fifteen minutes a chapter. 4. Math homework assignments took about one hour to do. I beat my time estimation. 5. Calling friends for math and study advice was very helpful. 6. I learned a lot from my teacher's email responses to my questions.	I was 100 percent successful in turning on and watching the video lectures on schedule.

Adjustments	None.	To make math more useful and interesting: 1. After each problem-solving session, I added watching a rerun of the TV show Numbers, which showed how you could solve mysteries with numbers. 2. I volunteered to do calculations at the animal shelter: I learned to do a chocolate toxicity calculation for a dog that ate part of a chocolate bar.	Adjusted time estimations.	1. When I delayed starting homework problems, I used the five-minute system to kick-start the process. 2. When I told myself I'd start later, I immediately labeled that procrastination thinking and went back to my plan.
Results		Calling friends for math and study advice was very helpful.	One and half hours for solving math problems was sufficient.	Five-minute plan was helpful for starting problem-solving session. Was about 90 percent consistent on implementing the plan.

Molly's written review affirmed that she could apply a self-regulated learning approach to master the course material in her toughest subject. She earned an "A" grade. That was another affirmation. However, conquering her fear of math was more important to her.

Here is Eagle's final note: "Results normally depend on the process that you follow. However, the outcome is not always going to be under your control. You organize a hike for your friends. On the day of the hike, there is a major thunderstorm. You cancel the hike. The process was under your control. The storm was not."

It's your turn to review the results of your self-regulated learning experiment.

Dimension	Goal Setting	Planning	Organizing	Implementing
Process				
Evaluation				
Adjustments				
Results				

Describe the results of your performance.

Your Progress Report

1. What three key ideas in this chapter struck you as most important to remember?

2. What three actions can you take to combat your target procrastination problem?

3. What resulted when you took these actions?

4. What did you learn from the actions?

5. What would you do differently next time?

chapter 8

Reducing Stress and Optimizing Performances

When stress accompanies change, procrastination is a familiar companion. In this chapter, you'll learn how to develop self-mastery skills for reducing stress and feeling more relaxed and ready to go. This sets the stage for procrastinating less. You'll specifically see how to (1) clear your mind by meditating, (2) relax your body with deep breathing exercises, (3) build emotional reserves with scenes for serenity, and (4) use the *ready, relax, set, go technique* to launch actions for peak performances. As you develop these skills, you put yourself in a strong position to bounce back faster from setbacks and to make positive changes in the way that you go about getting things done.

How Stress Strikes

When stressed, you are responding to a condition or change, often a negative one. You may feel stressed by unwanted noise, crowded conditions, or changing technologies that require rapid mental adjustments. You may have a series of challenging school assignments where you are uncertain about what to do. You also may impose stresses on yourself, such as forgetting to put an essay in your backpack or leaving late for school. You may be surprised to know that even positive changes increase your level of stress, such as starting your first year at a college of your choice.

When stressed, you are likely to put off doing things that will add to your stress, such as starting difficult and challenging learning assignments. If you put off too many things too often, you may feel stressed by tasks that are piling up. This is the *procrastination accumulation effect*. The more you leave not done, the more stressed you are likely to feel. When you feel stressed, you may procrastinate more. It's a vicious cycle.

You can't feel stressed out and relaxed at the same time. Can relaxing your mind and body prepare you to perform at higher levels and help you procrastinate less? Let's see.

Practicing Meditation

Meditation is the practice of training your mind to focus on a single word or object for a predetermined time. A primary purpose is to clear your mind of negative thoughts. Within about eight weeks, this method appears to bring about improvements in memory, learning, and perspective along with an increase in activity in the brain regions responsible for these functions.

At one time, you'd have had to pay a meditation guru hundreds of dollars for a mantra, or special word that you'd hum silently to yourself as you sat in a lotus position as you meditated. Humming the special word would bring you a feeling of peace and tranquility. However, there is nothing magical about a guru-provided word. Single-syllable words or sounds like "one" or "mmm" can produce a meditation effect.

There are many ways to meditate. Here's one: Put yourself in a comfortable and quiet place where you are safe from interruptions. It can be leaning against a wall, sitting in a comfortable chair, or sitting in a comfortable position. For five minutes in the morning and five minutes in the afternoon, silently hum a simple word, such as "one." If an intrusive thought pops to mind, don't sweat it. Imagine the thought drifting away in a cloud. Then continue to hum "one" silently to yourself.

If you choose, use the following to record what resulted.

Action	Short-Term Results (One Week) of Doing This Exercise Twice a Day	Long-Term Results (Eight Weeks) of Doing This Exercise Twice a Day
Meditation Experiment: Silently repeating a neutral single syllable word to yourself		

Deep Breathing

Deep breathing triggers a relaxation response. There are different ways to do this. Here is a deep breathing technique called square breathing: Put yourself in a comfortable position. Breathe through your nose, moving your chest and stomach at the same time. Over a four-second period, take a deep breath. As you breathe in, count from 1 to 4 in your mind. Wait two seconds. Then slowly release your breadth for about four seconds as you count "4, 3, 2, 1" in your mind. Wait two seconds. Keep repeating the cycle for two minutes.

The purpose of this exercise is to relax your body and lessen your general level of stress. If you have been putting off a school task, you may feel relaxed enough to start the task.

If you choose, use the following to record what resulted.

Action	Short-Term Results (One Week) of Doing This Exercise Twice a Day	Long-Term Results (Eight Weeks) of Doing This Exercise Twice a Day
Deep Breathing Experiment: Square Breathing		

Relaxing with Nature

Your brain processes certain pictures that you create in your mind in the same way as a live scene. Some scenes evoke pleasant feelings of serenity. Visualize yourself sitting on top of a large boulder. It's a warm day with white clouds scattered across a blue sky. You are aware of the sound of birds in the background. You look down at a stream cascading over rocks in a lightly wooded area with lots of open spaces and sunny areas. Your eye follows the stream to where it flows into a lake with waves lightly touching the shore. How do you feel?

Some scenes evoke a sense of strain. Imagine yourself looking at a mall parking lot filled with cars and SUVs. You see an empty fast food bag on the ground. You see people hurrying toward the mall entrance with a "50% Off Sale" banner over the door. You look to the sky and see dark clouds on the horizon. Do you feel any different from the scene you saw from the boulder?

Why do certain nature scenes have the power to evoke feelings of serenity? Our dominant sense is visual. Some nature scenes are visually pleasing and relaxing.

For this reason, people pay a premium to live where they can see the ocean, a lake, or other large body of water. Such scenes stimulate your brain's complex survival circuitry.

Nature scenes that suggest safety, security, and resources for surviving through thriving are inviting. Our ancient ancestors would approach these areas in preference to areas where predators could hide and where food and water looked scarce. In modern times, the early regions of your brain still respond to perceptions of these scenes by stimulating feelings of serenity.

There is abundant scientific evidence to show that daily exposure to nature scenes can reduce stress, improve your mood, extend your concentration, and add to your feelings of psychological well-being. As little as five minutes a day in nature helps promote this serenity effect.

What do you need to know about nature scenes to produce a serenity effect? Let's start with some critical features of a serenity scene:

- a clutter-free scene of open spaces that includes green areas and blue skies

- no signs of human-made structures or human presence—out-of-place objects can distract from the scene

- clear water in abundance

- complexity to stimulate curiosity, such as a stream winding into a plush, wooded area

You can evoke a serenity effect by visualizing a nature scene, viewing photographs of these scenes, or looking at live nature scenes. Experiment with the type of scene that you find most serene. Have one as the wallpaper on your computer screen. Spend some time in nature. Turn your bedroom into a nature scene with pleasing posters on the wall and plants on a windowsill. Your early brain regions will appreciate that, and you may feel rewarded with less stress.

Experiment with serene scenes and see if you feel more relaxed and productive more often. If you choose, use the following to record what resulted.

Action	Short-Term Results (One Week) of Doing This Exercise Twice a Day	Long-Term Results (Eight Weeks) of Doing This Exercise Twice a Day
Visualizing or Observing Serene Scenes (such as a photo of a seashore with islands in the background)		

The Ready, Relax, Set, Go Technique

You can optimize your performance with a self-mastery skill that follows a sequence of readying yourself by setting a goal, relaxing your body, mobilizing your mind, and launching an energized effort. This approach can help boost your performance in athletic contests, when speaking before a group, when interviewing with a college admissions officer, or when starting a homework assignment. Here's how:

Ready. Set meaningful, measurable, and reasonable goals. This is one of the most reliable ways to make progress. Working five minutes on a task is more reasonable than "getting everything done." If you feel stressed speaking up in class, asking a single question in a group setting is a reasonable goal. Take these types of steps repeatedly, and the odds are you'll feel confident asking questions in a group.

Relax. Put yourself in a relaxed state of mind. Pick the method that works best for you. It could be visualizing a calming nature scene, meditating, or deep breathing for two-minutes. When you feel calm, go to the next step.

Set. Prepare to act. In a relaxed state, keep your goal in mind. Then, think these three phrases to yourself: *I am feeling energized. I am ready to act. I will start now.* Repeat these self-instructional phrases four times.

Go. Launch goal-directed actions. Take the first step. Once you do this, you may find it easier to take the second.

What resulted from your *ready, relax, set, go* experiment? If you choose, use the following to record what resulted.

Action	Short-Term Results (One Week) of Doing This Exercise Twice a Day	Long-Term Results (Eight Weeks) of Doing This Exercise Twice a Day
Using the *Ready, Relax, Set, Go* Technique		

As you increase your ability to relax and mobilize, you may find that you automatically evoke this process when it is important to launch actions that lead to more accomplishments. This is called the *accomplishment accumulation effect.*

Your Progress Report

1. What three key ideas in this chapter struck you as most important to remember?

2. What three actions can you take to combat your target procrastination problem?

3. What resulted when you took these actions?

4. What did you learn from the actions?

5. What would you do differently next time?

chapter 9

Simplifying Your Decisions

Torn between a temptation and a loss, Michael couldn't decide what to do. He explained, "I felt stuck." Here was Michael's dilemma: He was attracted to Alice, a new girl in school. However, he was going out with Sophie, whom he had known since elementary school. He couldn't make up his mind. Should he ask Alice to go out with him? Should he break up with Sophie? What if he broke up with Sophie and Alice wouldn't go out with him?

Sophie knew Michael well enough to know that he was distancing himself from her. She dropped him. Before Michael introduced himself to her, Alice started dating someone else.

Michael made many minor decisions without hesitation. However, for major life decisions, he was often indecisive to the point of emotional paralysis. For example, he had trouble deciding whether to apply for an early admission decision to a college that interested him. He knew that early admission decisions were binding. He had no guarantee that he'd make the right choice. He procrastinated. Here's Michael's reason: "I'm afraid I'll make a mistake. What if I found out that I could have gotten into a better college?" Michael "decided" the early decision dilemma by delaying past the deadline.

Michael is not unique. From time to time, practically everyone hesitates too long on deciding some big and small matters: to hang out with friends or to study, to say what you think or stay silent, to take an SAT study course or not, or to go with "X" to the prom or with someone else.

Michael burdens himself with *decision-making procrastination*, which means he puts off making decisions until another day or time. He waits until the last minute to make a decision, decides too late, or waits until someone makes the decision for him.

In this chapter, we'll look at the role of emotions in decision making using a horse-and-rider metaphor to explore why people procrastinate on decision making and how to build decisiveness skills.

Emotions in Decision Making: The Horse and the Rider

Most dictionaries define the word "decision" as a process where you make a choice between two or more conditions after thinking it out. However, when you put off making decisions, why do you stop yourself from reasoning things out?

Decision-making procrastination has an emotional component that is connected to many thoughts and feelings, from worrying about failing to an aversion for uncertainty. Say you have a class presentation to make. You are afraid that if your presentation doesn't go well, your peers will judge you harshly. You feel tense every time you think of your presentation. To avoid thinking about it, you avoid preparing for it. You're so unprepared and anxious that you decide to skip school on the day of the talk. Ultimately, you based a series of procrastination decisions on avoiding anxiety from uncertainty, and this has led to a larger problem (the result of skipping school).

Some tough choices include unknowns. Under conditions of uncertainty, you'll sometimes make errors. If you think you need a guarantee that your decision will be right before you act, you might avoid a decision for as long as you can. Perhaps you'll make an impulsive decision to escape the tension of indecision. As you master decision-making skills, you can learn to accept uncertainty as you improve the timeliness and quality of your decisions. You can grow wise as you learn to make reasoned decisions.

How do you choose reason over impulse when decision-making procrastination seems to come naturally? If you've read novelist Rick Riordan's story *Percy Jackson and the Olympians*, or if you saw the movie, you met Chiron, a centaur—a being who is half-horse and half-human and who represents the very best of our animal and human natures. Chiron is a nurturing, patient, wise teacher with the ability to impart wisdom and encourage self-discovery. Perhaps Chiron has an answer.

The founder of psychoanalysis, Sigmund Freud, drew from the myth of the centaur to create a metaphor of a horse and rider. He did this to show the ongoing conflict between impulse and reason and how the conflict might be resolved. Let's start with the horse's perspective.

The horse is a creature of the moment with its own priorities. When it feels like it, the horse heads for the field to graze, the stream to drink, and the barn to sleep. It frolics. It runs with the other horses. When panicked, it bolts. The horse lives in the here and now and is not concerned with longer-term interests.

Your horse represents your passions, emotions, and impulses. The horse takes the path of least resistance. When the horse is in charge, you'll party rather than study for tomorrow's quiz.

Your rider is the executive of your destiny. Endowed with the powers of thought and perspective, your rider (a resident of the executive suite; see chapter 3) can transcend the boundaries set by the horse. However, your rider does not enter this world with all necessary worldly knowledge. At all stages of life, there is more to learn. For example, when you feel uncertain and confused, sorting things out is your rider's job.

Your rider has the power to accept responsibilities, act in an organized way, and work to achieve personal benefits and advantages. Your rider has the capacity to do things for the good of others. Among the rider's tools, you'll find the power of foresight, which allows you to look beyond the moment to see what is in your long-term interest to do. That's something that neither the horse nor the frog you met in chapter 3 can do. Faced with an upcoming test, an enlightened rider will take ample time to study.

When Horse and Rider Are in Conflict

Like Chiron, who balances the best of human and animal natures, the horse and rider will often work together. However, conflicts are inevitable. Your mind will sometimes tell you to do one thing as your emotions pull you in a different direction.

When you have something to do that is uncomfortable, your horse is inclined to make automatic procrastination decisions. These decisions can start with a negative perception of a task, negative feelings, and an urge to diverge into safer, easier, or more comfortable areas. Even a slight negative feeling can startle the horse into setting a procrastination process into motion. Unfortunately, the rider may be swayed by horse impulses and support them with a negative evaluation of the situation that spurs a procrastination outcome.

A double-agenda dilemma surfaces when the horse and rider pull in opposite directions. You have frustrating assignments to do. You have an urge to follow a procrastination path. At the same time, you want to achieve and succeed. You face a Y choice. The letter Y has two branches, much like a branch in a road. You can pause and ponder a direction, and go one way or the other, but you can't go in both directions at the same time.

Y decisions are a daily part of life. You have a math assignment, and you are not sure how to go about solving the problems. Your rider's goal is to do well on the assignment to get a better grade. Your horse has a different agenda, which is to avoid uncertainty and avoid feeling uncomfortable. This is your Y choice, and how you decide the issue predicts what happens next. Let's see how the rider and horse make choices when each works against the other.

Here is a rider's view of the Y choice: choose the most productive action even if it is uncomfortable, realizing that the discomfort will pass and solving the problem is more important than the initial discomfort. (Learning to bear discomfort, while striving to do better, is a sign of maturity. It's also a measure of resilience, or the ability to withstand adversity.)

Here is the horse's view of the Y choice: instead of thinking things through, you want to put this off because you want to avoid stirring up unpleasant emotions. Here is the horse's solution: take the path of least resistance, which is to put it off as long as you can. Meanwhile, the horse heads for the barn to eat hay.

Horse-and-rider conflicts are inevitable. Sometimes it is important for the rider to have a good grip on the reigns. The ordering-of-choice method can help.

The Ordering-of-Choice Method

When you know you are going to be pressed for time and it is important for you to stay focused, try an *ordering-of-choices method.*

Let's suppose that you pick getting good grades to get into a good college as your top "study priority." Your rider is interested in staying on track when you have a test, presentation, or paper to do. That's how you'll achieve your "good grades" objective. Your horse has a different idea: frolic, play, and avoid whatever feels uncomfortable. However, there is a time for play and a time for following through whether you feel uncomfortable or not. When you get this backward, you have a procrastination problem.

Here is how the rider can take charge. Organize your study activities into A, B, and C priorities. Priority A is a top-drawer activity, such as studying for a test scheduled for tomorrow. B, or middle-drawer, activities can wait, but not for long. Bottom-drawer activities are distractions that interfere with rational rider priorities. Here is an example:

Top Drawer	Midterm test tomorrow: review notes, text material, and sample questions Essay on assigned novel due in three weeks
Middle Drawer	Get daily chores done quickly Read a chapter a day and start outlining essay
Bottom Drawer	Tweeting, texting, and joining friends at the mall Organizing pencils by color, downloading apps, creating origami dragons, surfing the Internet

If you elevate a middle-drawer activity above a pressing priority, it is as much of a diversion as going to an office supply store to buy paper clips when you're running out of study time for tomorrow's test.

The ordering-of-choices method puts your choices into a sharp perspective. You'll know what distractions to avoid. You have a better chance of succeeding by sticking to priorities.

It's your turn to target what is most pressing and important from an enlightened rider's perspective.

Top Drawer	
Middle Drawer	
Bottom Drawer	

As you master the method, you'll find other ways to use this method of organizing priorities.

Practice Decision Making

Your decision-making skills may be the most important psychological tools that you have when it comes to living a happy, healthy, and productive life. Because making decisions happens so often in life, you'll have many opportunities to refine these skills. Here are a few common horse-and-rider conflicts that give opportunities for the rider to improve decision-making skills:

- sticking to your principles or going along with peer pressure to change them

- sharing how you feel or keeping a stiff upper lip

- studying for a test that can get you the grade that you want or going to a concert

- taking a part-time job to pay for a car or increasing the amount of time studying to get top grades so you can get into a top college

You know the results of procrastination. How can you put your enlightened rider in charge to sharpen your productive abilities in the above and other similar conflict situations?

Experiment: Put Yourself in Charge

What decision is a priority for you today that you've put off for too long? Describe it in the box below.

Now, try the following experiment for resolving horse-and-rider conflicts.

The chart shows both branches of the Y choice. The left column describes the rider's position, and the right describes the horse's. Under each example, fill in the blanks.

The Way of the Rider	The Way of the Horse
Define the problem by describing the rider's choices (such as waking up early to study, not going to the mall and studying instead).	Define the problem by describing the horse's choices (such as watching TV, checking social media, cleaning).

Look deeper at your choices. Identify the advantages and disadvantages of each.

_____

_____

_____

_____

Write what your horse is thinking to avoid working to solve the conflict. (Examples: _I'm too tired. I can't think about that now._)

_____

_____

_____

_____

Accept areas where there are unknowns and fill in the gaps where you can:

_____

_____

_____

_____

Engage in safe pursuits, such as playing video games. (List your distractions.)

_____

_____

_____

_____

Make decisions based on your best estimates for a favorable outcome. Think about executing the decision and imagine taking the first step:

_____

_____

_____

_____

Feel a sense of relief for temporarily avoiding what you find uncomfortable. (Describe what you gain and what you lose.)

_____

_____

_____

_____

The Way of the Rider	The Way of the Horse
Take the first step. What happens next?	Act hopeful, such as, "Perhaps I'll feel inspired later." What happens next?
What are the results of continuing to improve your decision-making skills?	What are the results of continuing with procrastination processes?

Once you map your Y-decision paths and compare them, you are in a position to make an informed decision on taking either the rider's or the horse's path. What path do you choose? Why?

Your Progress Report

1. What three key ideas in this chapter struck you as most important to remember?

1. What three actions can you take to combat your target procrastination problem?

2. What resulted when you took these actions?

3. What did you learn from the actions?

4. What would you do differently next time?

chapter 10

Using Time Effectively

In this chapter, you'll learn self-mastery skills for getting assignments done efficiently, meeting deadlines, and avoiding the needless hassles that so often go with doing things late.

Danny is a bright, affable teen who easily makes friends. If you needed help, you could count on him to be there for you right away. One other thing stands out about Danny. He routinely underestimates the time it takes to study. He avoids doing his assignments by doing other things instead. Thus, he normally turns in his school assignments late.

To deflect blame for his lateness, Danny kiddingly blames it on the clock. He has other more serious-sounding reasons: "I have too much to do." "It's boring." "It takes too long." "I'm not good at studying." However, the "I have too much to do" reason for delaying doesn't explain why he creates time to quickly help friends.

Danny's grades are mostly C's and D's with occasional B's and A's. However, compared to his college-bound peers, Danny performs above his peers on the history and math standardized achievement tests. (These are the tests where students from different schools answer the same questions.) For example, for every 100 people who took the same standardized history test, Danny scored higher than 99, but his history grade in school was D.

Why does Danny get such poor grades in school but do well on standardized tests? His pattern goes something like this: His mind often drifts when he is in class. He periodically watches the clock, hoping it will speed up so the school day can end. Thus, he misses a lot of what is going on in class. Because he drifts so often, he dreads his teachers calling on him to answer a question. He distracts himself with fear. To catch up, he does outside reading on the school subjects. These efforts are too late to help his grades but do help his standardized test scores.

Danny's self-initiated learning efforts are the actions of a person motivated to learn but whose grades can't benefit as he remains behind in his day-to-day studies and is graded down severely on his late or partially completed homework assignments. He will have to make some adjustments and compromises to improve his classroom performance.

Let's continue with Danny's story, when he meets a compassionate guide, the *Time Master.*

As he was sitting under an oak tree pondering his future, Danny heard a calm and confident voice. "I am the Time Master. Perhaps I can help you with your time problems."

Danny felt startled but not scared—and he was instantly curious. In a humorous way, he said, "Time is a problem for me. Can you get rid of all the clocks?"

An amused Time Master said, "You can't avoid time. Without a clock, your brain still keeps time. That is because your sense of time and timing is very important. Perhaps for this reason, time resides in many places in the brain.

"Different brain regions automatically calculate intervals, such as when you observe movement or hear sounds. Darkness and light trigger your circadian rhythms for sleep and wakefulness. Memorable times of your life reside in the hippocampus, a memory region in your brain. However, clock time is different. Among other things, the clock helps organize work and activities for people in complex societies. Your ability to interpret clock time resides in executive brain regions. You also use your executive functions to stay on course with your studies. However, executive controls over clock time will sometimes compete with your biological clock. How you resolve that will affect how you perform in your studies and other things in life where the clock competes with your natural time inclinations."

Boosting Productive Actions with Time Estimation and Planning

"Okay," Danny said, "How about doing some *time magic* and turn me into the best time manager ever."

The Time Master paused then said, "Interesting thought, Danny. Students who manage their time effectively perform well in their studies. So, learning time management (TM) methods makes sense. However, some scientific studies show that additional TM training (also study skills training) has a negligible effect on improving performances, especially when procrastination is an issue. That is because procrastination is an emotion-driven performance problem with time as a factor. Thus, time is a measure and a guide for quality performances. You create the performance.

"The solution for building better self-mastery skills is more about not procrastinating on using TM methods than using TM methods to overcome procrastination. However, you could try a new time management technique a week, such as taking five minutes before you go to bed to list tomorrow's priorities. A reminder can help. For example, set an alarm on your cell phone to ring at a certain hour each evening.

"You mentally make good time estimates every day. You know how long it takes to get from your home to school and from one class to another. You know about how long it takes to play your favorite video game. However, your timing on your schoolwork is different. You might try a different way if you are falling behind on your studies.

"Most people are overly optimistic about the time it takes to do any kind of schoolwork. False optimism is a common prelude for procrastination. For example, if you arbitrarily convince yourself that something won't take too long to do, it is easy to justify putting it off. You can recalibrate this thinking by working at making reasonably accurate time estimations for each phase of a project. By doing this, you increase the odds that you'll use your study time efficiently and not surrender to planning and counterfactual fallacies. (A fallacy is a false and misleading belief.)

"When you are overly optimistic about the time it will take to do something, it is an example of a *planning fallacy*. Misled by the fallacy, you may think you have plenty of time to get your schoolwork done. So you put off starting. After feeling frazzled by last-minute rushes to finish, you might think of how things could have been different if you had made another choice. This is the *counterfactual* fallacy, which means you think about something that you could have done but didn't. Since it didn't happen, it's counter to the facts.

"Planning fallacies and counterfactuals are like bookends separated by time and space. Because of this gap, you may not see the irony in telling yourself you have plenty of time in the beginning and then telling yourself you could have done better if you started earlier.

"With foresight about time estimations, you can avoid the procrastination bookend trap. You can start with comparing an 'I'll do it later' procrastination time plan with a concrete time estimate where you mentally break down an assignment and estimate the time it will take to do each part."

Danny said, "I have nothing to lose except the fallacies. But I still like the idea of getting rid of clocks."

Time Master continued: "Procrastination time estimates are often vague and noncommittal, and have negative results. Seeing through this self-deception is an advantage. Let's compare procrastination time estimates with productive time estimates. This can expose a fallacy and be a launching point for doing productive estimates."

Working with the Time Master, Danny created a two-column table to compare procrastination and productive time estimates and their probable results. He used his chemistry homework assignment for his test case.

Procrastination Time Estimates	Productive Time Estimates
I have plenty of time to do the chemistry assignment.	Break down chemistry homework assignment into its parts and estimate the time it will take to do each.
	Gather materials—book, worksheets, and calculator: 1 minute
	Read chapter 6: 40 minutes
	Answer questions: 7 minutes each for 7 questions
	Total time: 83 minutes
Estimate Procrastination Results	**Estimate Productive Results**
Being too optimistic and misjudging time leads to false confidence.	Have a more realistic perspective on the time the task will take.
Ran out of time and felt urgency.	Can better see that I need to find a specific time slot to do the assignment; leaving this up to chance won't work.
Frittered time with counterfactual "could have been" thinking.	
Asserted that next time I'll start early and study harder.	Starting sooner rather than later allows me to think about and to digest the information without feeling rushed.
Procrastination continues as before.	
Feel discouraged.	

When he created a time estimate for a chemistry assignment, and then matched it against his usual procrastination time estimations, Danny had an epiphany. Time is a measure of many things, including performance. By using time estimates for performance, he could match the estimate against the time it took him to perform the different parts of a task. To check the accuracy of his estimate, he'd have to do the task. With this perspective, he felt encouraged he could avoid the procrastination bookend trap. The next step was to translate feeling encouraged into action.

It's your turn to compare procrastination and productive time estimates and to explore the differences in results.

Your assignment: _____

Procrastination Time Estimates	Productive Time Estimates
Estimate Procrastination Results	**Estimate Productive Results**

The Easy-to-Difficult Sequencing Experiment

Time Master shared an observation. "Once you get the hang of making time estimates, you can combine this with an *easy-to-difficult sequencing technique,* which has some scientific backing. Starting easy takes less effort, depletes less energy, and is less stressful.

"Given a series of assignments, do the easy parts first. By starting this way, you create momentum for continuing. You may gain a triple benefit: (1) you are more likely to continue once you've started, (2) you make wiser use of your time, and (3) you avoid time conflicts."

Here is Danny's easy-to-difficult experiment for multiple homework assignments. He ordered the tasks from two of his classes according to how easy he believed the assignments would be. He added a time estimation dimension to get more practice judging the amount of time it takes to do an assignment.

Activity (Easiest First)	Time Estimation	Results
1. For English: Read Part 1 of "The Ancient Mariner" and answer assigned questions.	20 minutes for reading part 1 25 minutes for answering the questions 47 minutes total	25 minutes to read part 1 28 minutes to answer questions 53 minutes total Felt good about what I accomplished. Got questions 90 percent correct.
2. For chemistry: Study chapter 6 and answer questions at the end of the chapter.	30 minutes to read the chapter 7 minutes for each of the 7 questions, for a total of 42 minutes to answer them all 83 minutes total	Actual time: 25 minutes Actual time: 48 minutes Actual total time: 75 minutes Rechecked calculations. Got 100 percent correct on chapter questions.

When using this time estimation technique, Danny's grades improved to mainly B's and A's with an occasional C grade. When Danny got to college, he felt challenged and flourished. He graduated early in the top 1 percent in his class, attended graduate school, and earned a PhD.

You may have multiple tough assignments at the same time. Nevertheless, even the most difficult assignments have parts that are relatively easier to do. When in doubt about where to start, start "easy" and build from there.

Here is your easy-to-difficult experiment.

Activity (Easiest First)	Time Estimation	Results

What did you learn from this experiment? Record this information below.

Adjusting Your Inner Clock

If you are like many teens, you go to sleep later now than when you were a kid and you are likely to get less sleep than you need. If you have trouble falling asleep, sleep too long, or wake too early, you are likely to feel in a fog and feel half-asleep during your morning classes. You'll have difficulties concentrating and have a low tolerance for frustration. You are likely to feel overwhelmed by too many pressing academic responsibilities. A buildup of fatigue from lack of sleep may translate into lower grades than you are capable of attaining. You are also at a higher risk for sleep-related mood problems, weight gain, and impulsive reactions. This pattern may not be universal, but it is certainly common.

As a teen, your mental performance may peak between 1:00 and 7:00 p.m.—this is typical but there are plenty of exceptions. If high schools started later, you and most of your peers would be better off academically. However, you'll have less time for afterschool sports and other activities. A few schools make that tradeoff. Most don't.

Getting into a healthy sleep routine, such as sleeping between 11:00 p.m. and 7:30 a.m., helps calibrate your biorhythms and improves attention and concentration during school hours. This added sleep time can have an extra benefit. Your mind has quality time to consolidate learning. Even if you don't fall asleep at 11:00 p.m., relaxing your body has restorative value.

Cognitive behavioral methods, such as those you are learning in this book, are scientifically supported ways to improve your chances of sleeping well. Here are three cognitive behavioral techniques for sleep: (1) stimulus-control procedures, such as avoiding naps, going to bed only when sleepy, and using bed only for sleep; (2) relaxation methods, such as muscular relaxation, abdominal breathing, and creating pleasant, serene, mental images; (3) regulating your sleep by getting to bed and arising at uniform hours—even on weekends. Here are other ways of getting control over your sleep patterns:

- Omit things from your routine that contribute to wakefulness, such as eating before bed.

- Exposure to intrusive indoor light at night can have a suppressive effect on the hormone melatonin that helps trigger sleep. This includes light from your TV or computer screen. Avoid watching TV at least one half hour before your bed time.

- Avoid coffee, cola, tea, or chocolate (or other caffeine-containing substances) seven hours before your regular bedtime. The last thing you need is to feel charged up when the time comes for sleep.

- Sleep in a well-ventilated room with a room temperature of 65 to 68 degrees Fahrenheit. Sleep is associated with a drop in body temperature.

- Do moderate aerobic exercise during the afternoon every day. Most sleep experts suggest avoiding exercise two to four hours before you go to bed. Note: There is some research indicating that mild evening exercise at night aids sleep. Use your experience as a guide.

- Avoid associating your bed with wakefulness. When you are unable to sleep, get out of bed. Return in a few minutes. You may feel more ready to sleep.

- Deal with problems so you don't dwell on them when you are trying to sleep.

- If you have negative thoughts running through your mind at sleep time, imagine that they are like particles of dust in the wind. Imagine the wind scattering them about where they have no place to land. They are less oppressive when you don't struggle to suppress them.

- By procrastinating less, you'll have less to dwell on that can keep you awake.

Your Progress Report

1. What three key ideas in this chapter struck you as most important to remember?

2. What three actions can you take to combat your target procrastination problem?

3. What resulted when you took these actions?

4. What did you learn from the actions?

5. Specifically, what would you do differently next time?

chapter 11

Building on Your Gains

In this chapter, we'll explore three ways you can build on your gains: keeping yourself on track, following your enlightened values, and carving out a career direction that is compatible with your interests and abilities.

Keeping on Track

When you get to college, how you go about succeeding largely rests on your shoulders. You'll have support services to choose from, such as study skills programs. Whether you access them or not is your choice. The following four self-mastery skills are useful now, and they may be more useful when you get to college.

Assertiveness. If you quickly cave into pressure to do things for people just because they ask and then you end up in a bind, the word "no" is a short but helpful word. Knowing when to say no and when to firmly hold your ground is a useful skill.

Perspective. For major assignments (such as essays and term reports) that are due near final examination time, practice foresight. If you start earlier, you'll have more time to finish before the due date. That useful perspective can keep you from having too much to do when you have too little time to do multiple assignments well.

Efficiency. Find a way to use time when you are traveling to school on a bus, waiting in line, waiting in a doctor's office, going on a family trip, and so forth. When you get things done during these open periods, you'll have more free time later.

Free-time zones. A free-time zone is a time to do what you want, such as relax with friends, date, look at nature scenes, and so forth. If you have a tight schedule, you may need to formally schedule this into your routine. When you feel relaxed and mobilized to act, you've primed yourself for taking efficient and effective actions.

Exercising Your Positive Values

Can you leapfrog procrastination obstacles with your values as your guide? Let's take a brief look at values and see.

Your values are emotionally charged beliefs about what is important and where you stand on matters that concern you. Some are heavy duty guiding principles represented in words, such as "responsibility" and "integrity." Some are strong preferences, such as learning, friendship, or initiative. When you know where you stand on issues that matter, your values simplify your decisions.

Your values influence how you feel about and respond to situations. For example, you do the vast majority of the work on a group project, and all members of the group get equal credit. Do you think that's fair? However, there may be other issues, such as the desire to help friends. Given conflicting motives, your answer suggests the strength of your values for fairness or friendship in this situation.

Like lyrics in a musical recording, your values carry an emotional message. However, the volume of the message (loudness, softness, intensity) varies by situation, your perceptions, conflicting values, and general confidence in yourself to judge a situation accurately.

Can you choose your values? There is a precedent for doing this. For example, as a young adult, the famous eighteenth-century American scientist, inventor, and diplomat Ben Franklin devised and executed his own value system. He did this after a shaky transition into adulthood that included a number of poor decisions and failures.

Ben Franklin believed he needed a sound self-guidance system. After much thought—and feedback from others—he came up with thirteen guiding principles for building a *model self* that fit with his situation and times. He applied his value system to worthy goals and led a life that few could rival.

Let's get back to the question of whether you can leapfrog procrastination obstacles with values as your guide. It depends on the value, its amplitude, and conflicting issues. For example, a value for taking responsible actions conflicts with procrastination urges. If you follow through because it is the responsible thing to do, this value inhibits the procrastination urge. However, if responsibility is a low volume value, and if you have a high volume value goal for college, and if you have frequent procrastination urges, you'd wisely consider how to boost the volume on responsibility.

Exercising positive values for leapfrogging procrastination is a three-step process. You recognize when your procrastination urges can cascade into a procrastination cycle. Let's say the situation is a study assignment. Ask yourself, "Is following through on the assignment the responsible thing to do?" If you answer yes, you may experience just enough inner emotional pressure to execute a value for responsibility.

Finding a Career Direction

The world of work is an evolving place. Few stick with career choices they once thought about as children.

Some of the inner pressures when you get to college may center on deciding your major and preparing for a career. Maybe you can bypass that pressure with the self-mastery skills you are developing and additional knowledge of how your talents and interests line up with career options that are positive for you.

Knowing thyself helps when it comes to making an enlightened career decision. If you have already decided on a career, a career review is also a useful way to confirm or disconfirm a choice.

You can find over 12,000 career titles in the *Dictionary of Occupational Titles,* from abalone diver to zoo veterinarian. So how do you choose? Career selection is often a funnel-down process where you test one thing and then another, and narrow things down until you find the career direction that you prefer. As you explore your career options, you'll weed out some and add others. Here are some guidelines on streamlining a funnel-down process:

Accept uncertainty. The world of education and career options are changing. There is no guarantee you'll find an ideal direction. However, by doing your career homework, you load the dice in your favor.

Know yourself. As a starting point, look at careers that fit with areas where you get your highest grades. Then get a sense of your strengths, weaknesses, limitations, and opportunities in careers that appeal to you.

Use what you know. Apply what you learned about self-regulated learning to a career search. Set exploration goals, such as looking into social sciences one week then engineering the next. Execute the plan. Review what you learned. That's one way to funnel down on a career choice.

Read actively. Explore career options by reading career literature, reading short stories about what people do in different careers, reading people's career biographies, and so forth.

Work with others. Do career planning with a parent(s), a guidance specialist in career planning, and peers who are seriously seeking to find directions in the world of work. Ultimately, reserve the final decision for yourself.

Actively test careers that may interest you. Do volunteer work in promising areas. Shadow an expert who does what you think you might want to do. If you are interested in journalism, write for your school newspaper. If you find something you look forward to doing, you may have found a career niche area.

Maintain an adaptable career view. You may decide your preferred career direction in high school. You may change your mind when you get to college. Some new career options may emerge after college.

Look to the future. A longer-term time perspective on picking a career correlates with positive school achievement.

Developing Career Choice Confidence

An important piece to the puzzle of having a rewarding career is largely a function of being able to do what you prefer to do under preferred work conditions. Start this phase of the funnel-down process by matching your preferred work activities, preferred people conditions, and preferred work settings against job functions and conditions for careers that you are exploring. Here is how to do a preferred-work-environment assessment: (You'll probably make changes in these as you learn more about your capabilities and career options.)

1. What do you like to do (preferred activities)? For example, do you prefer to solve problems, work with mechanical devices, develop and test new ideas, organize the work of others, or do a combination of some of these things or something else? List these preferred activities below.

2. Under what people conditions do you work best? Do you prefer to work by yourself? Do you enjoy working and communicating with people? Do you prefer a balance between working with others and doing things on your own? Describe your preferred work conditions below.

```

```

3. Under what work settings do you believe that you'll feel more comfortable and confident? Do you prefer to work in a setting where you can predict what will happen next? Do you like changing circumstances that require solving problems? Do you prefer settings where you have the freedom to take initiatives? Describe your preference(s) below.

```

```

A strong career direction may amplify your intentions to do what you need to do to achieve your career objective. Even a tentative career direction can be an incentive for performing efficiently and effectively in your academics in high school and later in college. This incentive can favorably compete with procrastination urges, thinking, and behaviors.

Your Progress Report

1. What three key ideas in this chapter struck you as most important to remember?

2. What three actions can you take to combat your target procrastination problem?

3. What resulted when you took these actions?

4. What did you learn from the actions?

5. What would you do differently next time?

chapter 12

Twelve Things to Know Before College

When you want to figure something out, it normally helps to talk to sensible people with different perspectives. In this chapter, you'll find tips from twelve people with different perspectives on what you need to know about college before you get to college. I'll add a concluding remark.

1. Build on Your Strengths

The transition from high school to college is one of the biggest moves in life you'll ever make; the decisions you will make are so important. Base your decisions as much as possible on your self-knowledge—that is, who you are. If you see yourself as a risk-taker, consider a college that is farther away from home, perhaps in the heart of a big city, but if you are risk-averse, perhaps stay close to home and consider a college in a sleepy suburb or small town. Adapting your many decisions to who you are and what you know about yourself should make you happier and more effective when your college career kicks off. Think deeply about *your* academic and career interests, not so much what someone else wants you to do. Act upon your dominant interests, letting them influence your decisions about what college to attend and what strengths each college has relevant to those interests.

—Frank Farley, PhD, Former President of the American Psychological Association; L. H. Carnell Professor in the College of Education and Leadership Professor in the Department of Psychological, Organizational, and Leadership Studies; Temple University

2. Have Faith in Yourself

Whether we have psychological pain is not fully up to us, but how we respond to it is. The problem you will need to face in your life is this: when you encounter a painful challenge, your logical, problem-solving mind will very likely tell you to run, fight, or hide. Decades of research shows that these are the three worst things you can do. Pain is normal. In your future you may do poorly on a test; you may be rejected in love; you may lose a competition. You will hurt. If you turn toward pain— in a mental posture that metaphorically puts your arms wide, yours hands free, and your eyes open—you can feel, see, and learn from it. Buried inside pain is caring. Inside the pain of rejection is the yearning to be loved. Inside the pain of failure is the yearning to succeed. If you keep faith in yourself and let painful challenges teach you, you will learn more of what you care about, and gradually you will get better in achieving it. That lesson will be missed entirely if you run, fight, and hide, and that is a cost that is just entirely too high.

—Steven C. Hayes, PhD, Professor, University of Nevada; Author of *Get Out of Your Mind and Into Your Life*

3. Study with Flexibility

If there's coursework you dread, text yourself a "start up and get it done" date. To use this technique, give yourself a specific day and time you'll start the assignment and make a commitment to yourself to start at that time. Then keep your commitment. By taking a few seconds to text yourself, you can put a halt to endlessly saying, "I'll do it later." Moreover, just scheduling your study time can feel calming.

Life is fluid. So give yourself flexibility. If your car breaks down or you have an unexpected emergency club meeting, text yourself about your study time revision. Start as soon as possible.

Where you study can make a big difference. Select study spaces that you like. If you appreciate silence, try your desk or the library. If you prefer more stimulation, try a park or coffee shop. Mentally think of these go-to study spots when you have an assignment. Train your mind to associate these locations with productivity.

—Brittany Clifford, Honors Student, Southern Methodist University, Dallas, Texas

4. Diary of a Successful Student

When I got to college, I struggled because I had not developed good note-taking and study skills. I learned by watching what successful students did, and I tried out their methods. If it worked for me, I continued using it. Here are a few of the techniques that got me through college with a 4.8 GPA.

I read the assigned readings and did the homework according to the syllabus. When a test or quiz was a day or two away, I reread the material, took notes, and reviewed the class notes. If sample quizzes were available, I took them and checked my answers. In areas where my answers were incorrect, I went back to the readings and notes to review.

Then I would retake a random assortment of quizzes, including the ones I had not done well on before.

With regard to papers, I did the research early on and compiled it. When I felt that I knew enough about the topic, I wrote my paper.

My studies were not my life. I joined a number of organizations and attended every football game, dance, and concert. I studied during the week so I didn't need to study much on the weekends. I didn't feel deprived; I got what I needed to do done. During midterms and finals, I used my reading days to study.

I used the same skills for grad school and added a to-do list. I wrote down what I needed to do in a time frame and crossed out what I completed. It felt good crossing out items!

—Nancy Knaus, MBA, PhD, Coauthor of *Fearless Job Hunting*

5. Time Yourself for Success

When you have an unpleasant task to start, how about using your timer to kick start yourself into action? Here's how:

1. Set your timer for five minutes. That's the amount of time you'll work. Tell yourself, "If, after five minutes, I want to stop, I'll stop. If I really want to continue after that, fine, but it's not required!"

2. Work as quickly as you can to finish your task within the five minutes.

3. When the timer goes off, decide whether to continue or stop. Either way, you win!

4. Admire what you've completed! Tell yourself, "Even if I'll have more to do later, I can enjoy the feeling of accomplishment now!"

—Pamela D. Garcy, PhD, Success Coaching and Training, Dallas, Texas

6. Strike Out Your Procrastination Heavy Hitter

Why would smart students, who sincerely want to succeed in their academics, spoil their chances? The barrier is normally not intellectual but psychological.

Procrastination comes about for different reasons, such as low self-efficacy, proximity of temptation, the discomfort you associate with the task, or the belief that you can do it later. If you choose to change, start with your *heavy hitter*. This is what drives your procrastination habit more than anything else.

Discomfort-dodging procrastination is a common heavy hitter. You believe an assignment is too difficult, time consuming, or boring. You don't feel like doing the assignment and you give yourself permission to put it off as long as you can. If you don't like the results, experiment with the "so-what" technique where you reframe the situation. For example, "So what if I do not feel like doing something unpleasant. If I prefer to do well, rather than fall short, I'd better do it." Accept responsibility for your own changing, and your heavy hitter will have fewer times at bat.

—Michael Wald, EdD, School Psychologist, Somers Public Schools, Somers, Connecticut

7. Stay the Course

Life has a way of trying to distract us from our goals. It feels more comfortable to procrastinate on our work. But instant comfort does not go with success, so we need to choose. We try to choose success over comfort every time because success is a goal of ours and instant comfort is not.

Goals and good intentions are not enough—to succeed, we need strategies, and we would like to share some of them here. We observe ourselves to see which distractions divert us from success; if the distractions are truly enjoyable and worthwhile, we schedule them—

after the work is done—and enjoy them. We try to take on courses and tasks that we like; even if the work is hard, the motivation to do it comes readily. Perhaps most importantly, when we have a task that's boring, difficult, or unpleasant, we double our efforts. Success comes from doing things you don't feel like doing, when you still don't feel like doing them.

Our wish to succeed is fair and reasonable. A true friend does not knowingly try to divert us from a success path. We politely turn down offers that interfere with success. We also want to live full, balanced lives, with health, friends and family, fun, giving, personal growth, and relaxation. Sometimes, we feel like doing something that doesn't fit our goals at all, and that's where attitude and self-discipline come in. We have many tools for success, but procrastination is not one of them. By keeping up with our work, we can fully enjoy our other activities.

—Leah Altrows and David Altrows, Senior High School Students, Kingston Collegiate and Vocational Institute, Kingston, Ontario, Canada. (Their father, Irwin Altrows, PhD, is a clinical psychologist.)

8. Pit Conscientiousness Against Procrastination

When you procrastinate to avoid an uncomfortable assignment, your success is temporary. Eventually you'll feel a gnawing negative feeling as you are running out of time. If you often find yourself in this predicament, you risk bringing this habit to college.

High school is a good place to develop conscientiousness skills to replace procrastination habits. These skills go beyond budgeting your time, controlling procrastination impulses, and attending to the daily details of life. Acting conscientiously includes taking responsibility for your physical health by getting adequate sleep, eating a healthy diet, exercising, and avoiding the use of addictive substances that can sabotage your academic performances.

When you procrastinate on acting conscientiously, you avoid taking actions to achieve productive goals. However, procrastination is often the result of self-deception. You think you are really getting things done by making lists of what you are not doing, complaining to others about having an arduous schedule, devouring comfort foods when stressed by your studies, or waiting for the right feeling or mood to strike. Make yourself aware of these deceptions and you are on your way to acting conscientiously. Focus on the tasks you need to complete. Then make plans that break down what you need to do into workable steps on a timeline. Follow those instructions. That's the responsible thing to do.

—Michael F. Shaughnessy, PhD, and June Shepherd, PhD,
Eastern New Mexico University, Portales, New Mexico

9. Treat Procrastination with Compassion

Is it possible to give yourself a hopeful message for freedom from the burdens of procrastination? Try this meditation approach and see.

Start by sitting in a quiet, comfortable, place. Close your eyes and create a picture of yourself sitting across from yourself. As you take ten deep breaths to clear your mind and relax your body, watch the image of yourself breathe in, breathe out, and relax in unison. Continue deep breathing and silently say this to yourself: "May I be peaceful, happy, safe, and free from suffering the burdens of procrastination." Repeat the phrase, "May I be peaceful, happy, safe, and free from suffering the burdens of procrastination."

Now, switch images. Close your eyes and create a picture of a person whose procrastination is a burden to him or her. It can be a teacher, a friend, a parent—even someone you don't know well. Breathe in and breathe out as before. As you imagine the person sitting across from you, repeat this phrase two times: "May you be peaceful, happy, safe, and free from the burden of procrastination.

—Jon Carson, PsyD, and Matt Englar-Carson, PhD,
Authors of *Adlerian Psychotherapy*

10. Play a Game with Procrastination

Since teenagers spend an inordinate amount of time playing video games, here's a tip to overcome procrastination about writing an essay. Every time you destroy an enemy on your video game, turn to your laptop and write one sentence of your essay. Every time you lose a weapon or one of your avatars is destroyed, turn to your laptop and write three sentences. Try variations of this approach. Of course the idea is to tie a less desirable activity to a high frequency and desirable activity.

—Barry Lubetkin, PhD, ABPP, Founder, Institute for Behavior Therapy, New York City, Author, *Why Do I Need You to Love Me in Order to Like Myself* and *Bailing Out*

11. Think Proactively

Avoid a defeatist attitude: "No matter what I do I'm going to fail." "If I don't study, I'll fail, and if I study, I'll still fail." "Damned if I do, and damned if I don't!" Think proactively instead: "If I am to pass this course, I need to know x, y, and z. So, if I spend an hour or so on each, I should do reasonably well." Then put your plan into practice. Do something about it; don't simply paint yourself into a corner!

—Elliot D. Cohen, PhD, Author, *The Dutiful Worrier: How to Stop Compulsive Worry Without Feeling Guilty*

12. Know Yourself

Is procrastinating working for you or holding you back? Do you finish things on time, feel happy with the outcomes, and successfully manage the stress of being down to the wire? Can you take back control when needed?

If you answered yes, it is possible procrastination is a strategy you use to get things done more efficiently, pump up motivation, or create achievable challenge. Be careful with overusing this strategy or it will catch up with you!

If you answered no, procrastination is a failure to self-regulate your learning. (1) Weak task understanding leads to procrastination: What are you being asked to do? *Why* are you being asked to do it? It is easy to put work off when you are unsure about it. (2) Weak goals lead to procrastination: start with a CAST goal for a single one-hour study session. Be specific about (a) the *concepts* you need to know or use, (b) the cognitive *actions* or ways you need to know it (apply, compare, explain, etc.), (c) the *standard* you can use to self-evaluate (for example, I know it if I can explain it to my mom), and (d) commit to a specific *time* and duration to achieve this goal (for example, within one hour starting immediately after my lecture). It is easier to get down to work when you know exactly what you need to know and accomplish!

—Allyson F. Hadwin, PhD, Associate Professor of Educational
　　Psychology and Leadership Studies, University of Victoria, Canada

Believe in Yourself

When you were a kid, you may have watched the movie *Kung Fu Panda*. It was a story of Po, a klutzy panda, who endured tough training and overcame many obstacles to learn kung fu. He then used his natural talents and acquired skills to defeat Tai Lung, a powerful, evil snow leopard with a grudge. Tai Lung intended to take possession of a dragon scroll that contained a secret that would bestow limitless power on who possessed it. When Po got the scroll, and unrolled it, he looked and saw his own reflection. Po figured it out. When Tai Lung saw the scroll, he didn't get it. The secret of the scroll is to believe in yourself and to believe in what you can do.

Acknowledgments

My thanks go to the following professors, psychologists, teachers, school principals, and students who contributed wonderful ideas for this book: David Altrows; Leah Altrows; Irwin Altrows, PhD; Jon Carson, PsyD; Matt Englar-Carson, PhD; Brittany Clifford; Elliot D. Cohen, PhD; Allyson F. Hadwin, PhD; Frank Farley, PhD; Pamela D. Garcy, PhD; Steven C. Hayes, PhD; Nancy Knaus, MBA, PhD; Barry Lubetkin, PhD; Ann Scotten, MA; Greg Scotten, PhD; Michael F. Shaughnessy, PhD; June Shepherd, PhD; Michael Wald, EdD.

William J. Knaus, EdD, is a licensed psychologist with more than forty-six years of clinical experience working with people suffering from anxiety, depression, and procrastination. He has appeared on numerous regional and national television shows, including *The Today Show*, and more than 100 radio shows. His ideas have appeared in national magazines such as *U.S. News & World Report* and *Good Housekeeping*, and major newspapers such as *The Washington Post* and the *Chicago Tribune*. He is one of the original directors of postdoctoral psychotherapy training in rational emotive behavior therapy (REBT). Knaus is the author or coauthor of over twenty books, including *The Cognitive Behavioral Workbook for Anxiety*, *The Cognitive Behavioral Workbook for Depression*, and *The Procrastination Workbook*.

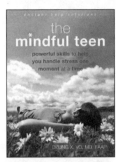

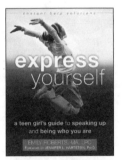

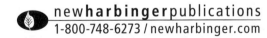

Register your **new harbinger** titles for additional benefits!

When you register your **new harbinger** title—purchased in any format, from any source—you get access to benefits like the following:

- Downloadable accessories like printable worksheets and extra content

- Instructional videos and audio files

- Information about updates, corrections, and new editions

Not every title has accessories, but we're adding new material all the time.

Access free accessories in 3 easy steps:

1. Sign in at NewHarbinger.com (or **register** to create an account).

2. Click on **register a book**. Search for your title and click the **register** button when it appears.

3. Click on the **book cover or title** to go to its details page. Click on **accessories** to view and access files.

That's all there is to it!

If you need help, visit:

NewHarbinger.com/accessories

new harbinger
CELEBRATING
40 YEARS